TABLE OF CONTENTS

LIST OF FIGURES

LIST OF TABLES

THIS PAGE INTENTIONALLY LEFT BLANK

LIST OF ACRONYMS AND ABBREVIATIONS

2-D	two-dimensional
3-D	three-dimensional
AEA	airborne electronic attack
API	application programming interface
COTS	commercial-off-the-shelf
CPU	central processing unit
DLL	dynamic-link libraries
DOD	Department of Defense
DTED	digital terrain elevation data
Elev.	elevation
EOB	enemy order-of-battle
EAPPO	Electronic Attack Platform Placement Optimization
ETIRMS	EA-6B Tactical Information and Report Management System
GPU	graphics processing unit
IADS	Integrated Air Defense System
IDE	integrated development environment
JATO	Jammer Technique Optimization
LOS	line-of-sight
MS	Microsoft
NAS	naval air station
NAVAIR	U.S. Naval Air Systems Command
NGA	National Geospatial Intelligence Agency
NGJ	Next Generation Jammer
PE	protected entity
PMA	Program Management Activity
TCP	Transport Control Protocol
VBA	Visual Basic for Applications

THIS PAGE INTENTIONALLY LEFT BLANK

EXECUTIVE SUMMARY

The research described in this thesis focuses on using pre-approved Department of Defense (DOD) software for developing military-specific applications. Traditional DOD software development models struggle to keep pace with emerging mission requirements of the modern battlefield. To combat this problem, the proposed solution tailors pre-approved, readily available commercial software to quickly develop military applications. Specifically, the limitations of using Microsoft Office, Adobe Acrobat, Internet Explorer, and Windows Applications Programs Interface (API) to meet complex military software requirements in the tactical environment were explored in this thesis.

The chosen test application to prove the viability of this approach is pictured in Figure 1. Currently, there is no software available to the warfighter capable of providing an optimal Airborne Electronic Attack (AEA) position against an enemy's complex Integrated Air Defense System (IADS). AEA operators must rely on their experience to determine the proper placement of their aircraft to best protect the bombing aircraft, or protected entity (PE), along the intended flight path. The emitter alignment criteria calculations required to successfully jam radars are too difficult and time consuming to be done manually in the allotted mission planning time. Continually changing mobile radar location updates only exacerbates this problem. The goal of the developed software is to automate this entire process.

Using only Microsoft Excel, its proprietary packaged scripting language Visual Basic for Application (VBA) readily available on most DOD computers, we developed an algorithm to automate the aforementioned task in software. Ambitious development and research led to an animated enemy order-of-battle (EOB) display pictured in Figure 2. Challenges overcome in the application include terrain and jamming impacted radar range (shown as range rings), PE and AEA route plotting, and emitter database processing. The successful results of this application validate the possibility of tailoring off the shelf, readily available software to build complex military specific applications.

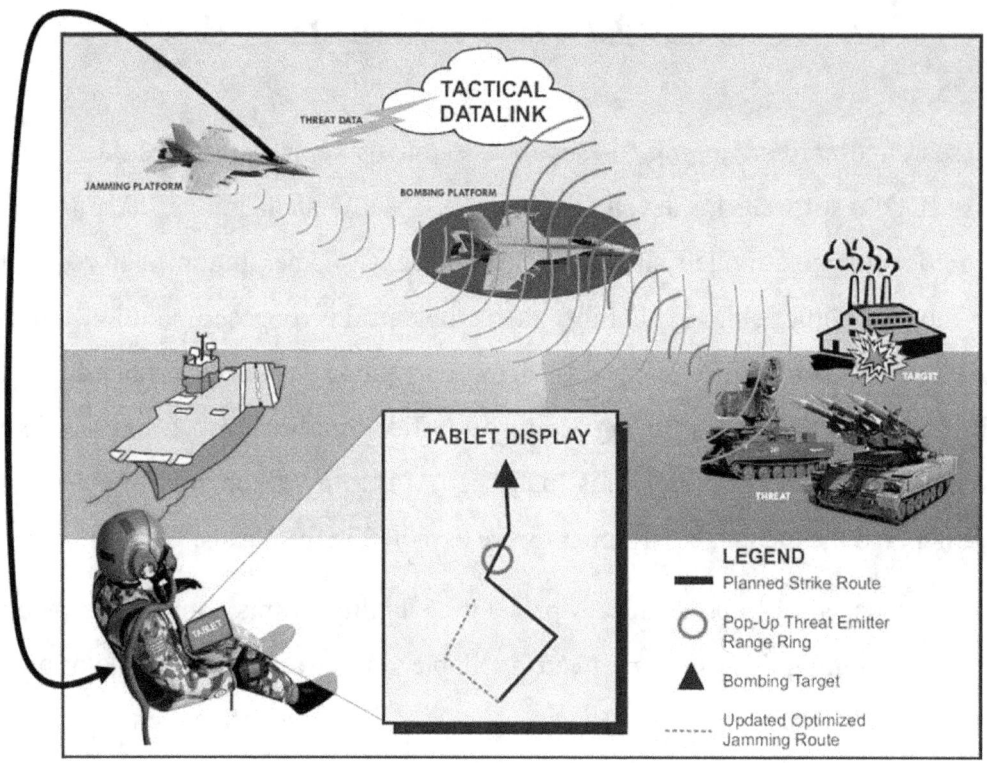

Figure 1. Operation View (OV) 1 chart depicting the proposed thesis software application developed using on pre-approved DOD software.

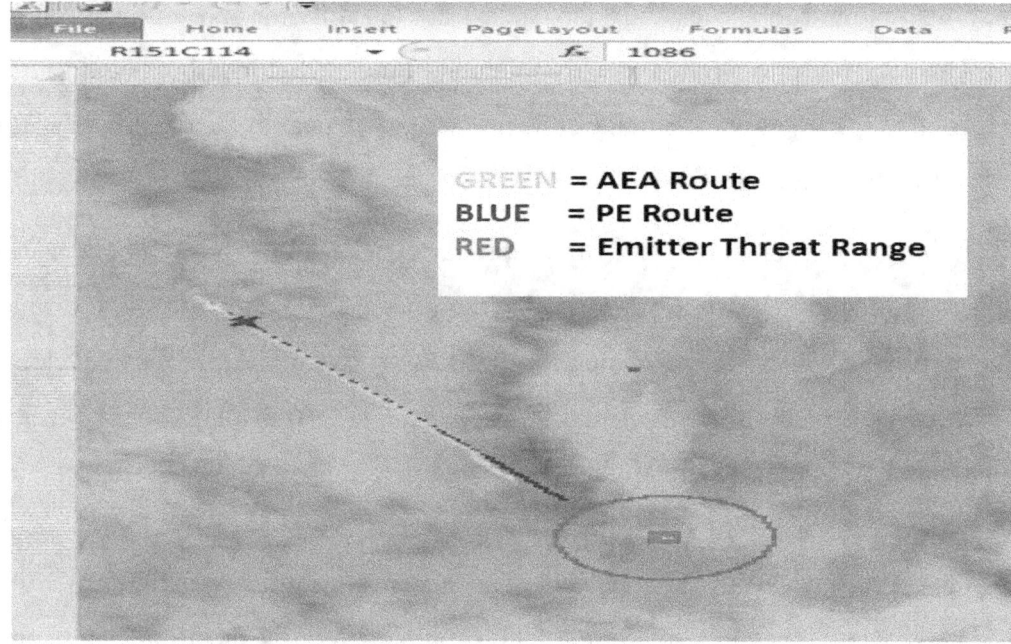

Figure 2. A screenshot of the software output displaying the automated optimized AEA jamming route and other overlays described in the legend.

I.   INTRODUCTION

The modern battlefield is an extremely complex and dynamic environment. Operator requirements are constantly changing to meet emerging threats. Traditional Department of Defense (DOD) software development techniques struggle to keep pace with the evolving threat. Rigorous Information Assurance (IA) requirements to combat the growing cyber threat further exacerbate the problem. The challenge is to develop an alternative to traditional software development models that can meet the operator and warfighter requirements without bypassing current rules and regulations mandated by law.

On such alternative is proposed in this thesis. The alternative proposed is the use of pre-approved, licensed software to develop military—specific applications. Specifically, the research sought to answer the question, can Microsoft (MS) Office, Adobe Acrobat or any other application approved for use on DOD networks be tailored to decrease the software development time, specifically the IA validation process, to help the warfighter in combat?

A.   ELECTRONIC ATTACK PLATFORM PLACEMENT OPTIMIZATION

An operational requirement was needed to test the validity of creating military-specific applications using only pre-approved software. The chosen application is the electronic attack placement platform placement optimization (EAPPO) algorithm. EAPPO was chosen to meet a capabilities gap for the airborne electronic attack (AEA) community. Currently, AEA mission planners do not have software available to assist in determining their optimal placement against an enemy integrated air defense system (IADS). AEA planners must rely on their operational experience and training to provide a best guess as to where the AEA asset needs to be in relation to the protected entity (PE) against the enemy IADS.

With the pending approval for AEA aircrew to carry tablets in their respective cockpits, the proposed software solution could eventually be expanded to provide real-time jamming optimization calculations to aircrew to combat the increasing mobile radar

1

threat. The high-level operational view chart (OV-1 for DOD Acquisitions) for the proposed software is displayed in Figure 1.

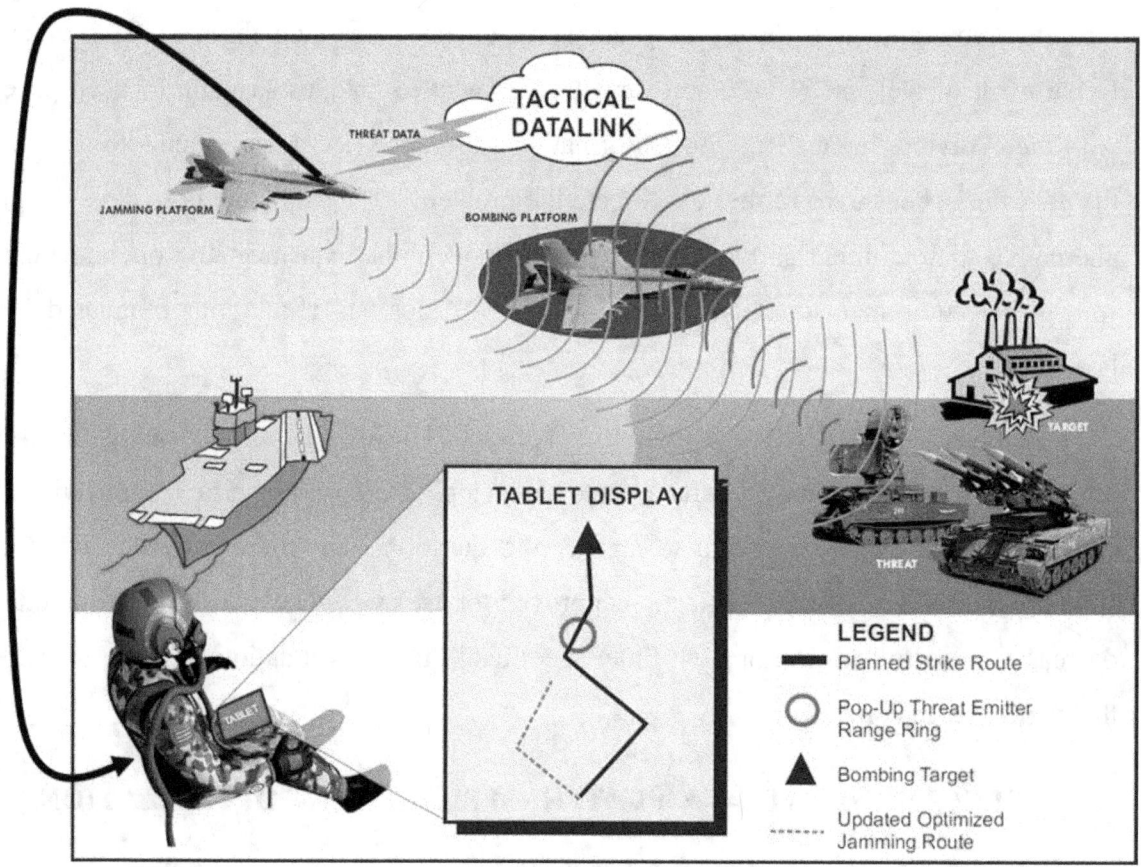

Figure 1.   Operation View (OV) 1 chart depicting the proposed thesis software application developed using only pre-approved DOD software.

B.   PRINCIPAL CONTRIBUTIONS

The two principal contributions of this thesis are the validation of using pre-approved software to develop military—specific applications and the development of EAPPO to meet a warfighter capability gap. Challenges encountered and examined in this thesis include:

- Development of a graphical user interface (GUI);

- Importing and analyzing digital terrain elevation data (DTED);

- Importing enemy order-of-battle (EOB) and corresponding jammer techniques;

- Developing optimization techniques for determining optimized AEA placement;

- Microsoft (MS) Excel animation;

- Using the graphical processing unit (GPU) from MS Office;

- Calling MS Windows application programing interfaces (API) from MS Office.

First, a GUI is needed to provide the look and feel of modern software by providing user-friendly software interfaces. Second, EAPPO needed the ability to import DTED data to produce radar terrain masking and grayscale map features. Third, EOB emitter parameters, locations, and jammer techniques needed to be imported from external sources to calculate how the jamming impacted emitter ranges (show as range rings). Fourth, optimization techniques needed to be developed and implemented to determine optimal AEA placement along the PE route. Fifth, EAPPO required animation to simulate its results to the operator. Sixth, details for the use of a GPU to augment the MS Office serial programming limitations are provided. Finally, this thesis discusses the ability of MS Office to integrate with Windows API functions by setting up a client-server application using two separate computers connected via WI-FI is discussed.

Although not a comprehensive list of possible features required for military software, the obstacles overcome in this study prove the feasibility of developing complex military applications using pre-approved software. Additionally, the completed EAPPO software can provide invaluable situational awareness to the warfighter, potentially saving aircraft and aircrew from perilous enemy weapon systems.

C.   THESIS OVERVIEW

This thesis contains five chapters starting with the Introduction in Chapter I. In Chapter II, the mathematics and algorithms specifically developed for EAPPO are presented. The EAPPO program execution is featured in Chapter III, using screenshots to demonstrate the software functionality and features. The EAPPO simulation results using test-emitter performance parameters and a PE strike route input by the warfighter is contained in Chapter IV. Finally, this thesis closes by drawing conclusions and making continued research recommendations in Chapter V.

II. APPLICATION DESIGN CHALLENGES AND DEVELOPED ALGORITHMS

The conceptual program flow for the jamming optimization application is displayed in Figure 2. The details of the application are provided in this chapter. To accomplish this task, this chapter is delineated into seven major sections. The seven major sections are:

- Pre-approved software selection;

- Radar and jamming fundamentals;

- Program input;

- Software algorithms;

- AEA optimization algorithm;

- Moving map in MS Excel;

- GPU and Windows API augment capabilities.

Basic details about the software environment chosen to develop the EAPPO application, MS Visual Basic for Applications (VBA), are provided in the first section. With an eye to radar jamming fundamentals, the foundations of radar beam forming and jamming for use in the software algorithm section are provided. Next, details for obtaining the required software inputs outlined in Figure 2 are provided in the program input section. After that, the details of EAPPO algorithm used to obtain the two application outputs are discussed in the software algorithms section. The developed software algorithms are tied into a flowchart depicting the necessary calculations determining optimal AEA location in the AEA optimization section. Next, the procedure for creating a moving map in MS Excel used to run the jamming simulation is discussed. Finally, Chapter II ends with a discussion on using a GPU and the Windows API to augment EAPPO.

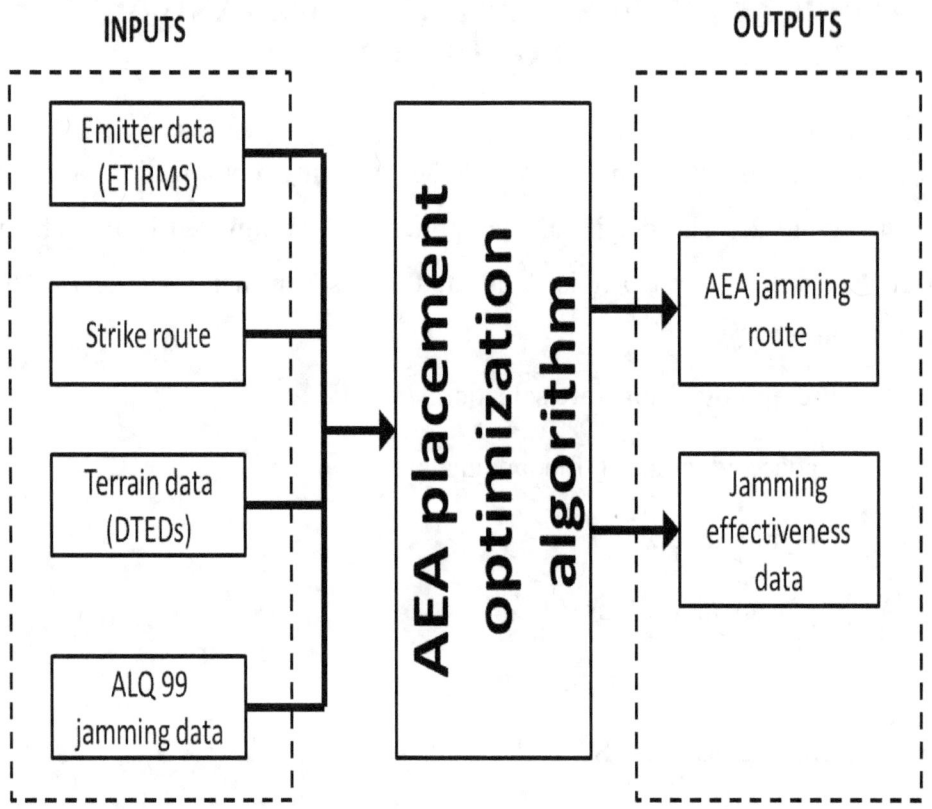

Figure 2.   The desired software inputs and outputs needed to run a jamming optimization program.

A.   VISUAL BASIC FOR APPLICATIONS

The pre-approved software constraint led to EAPPO being developed in MS VBA. VBA is a powerful automation tool built into all MS Office products. Based on the MS Visual Basic high level computing programming language, VBA is an object oriented program language with the ability to create user-defined functions as well as access Windows application programming interface (API) functions and other low level dynamic-link libraries (DLLs). The VBA integrated development environment (IDE) is available from any opened MS Office product by pressing Alt + F11. Figure 3 is a screenshot of the VBA IDE opened from MS Excel. The high proliferation of code snippets and tutorials on the web made it an excellent choice for the development of EAPPO.

6

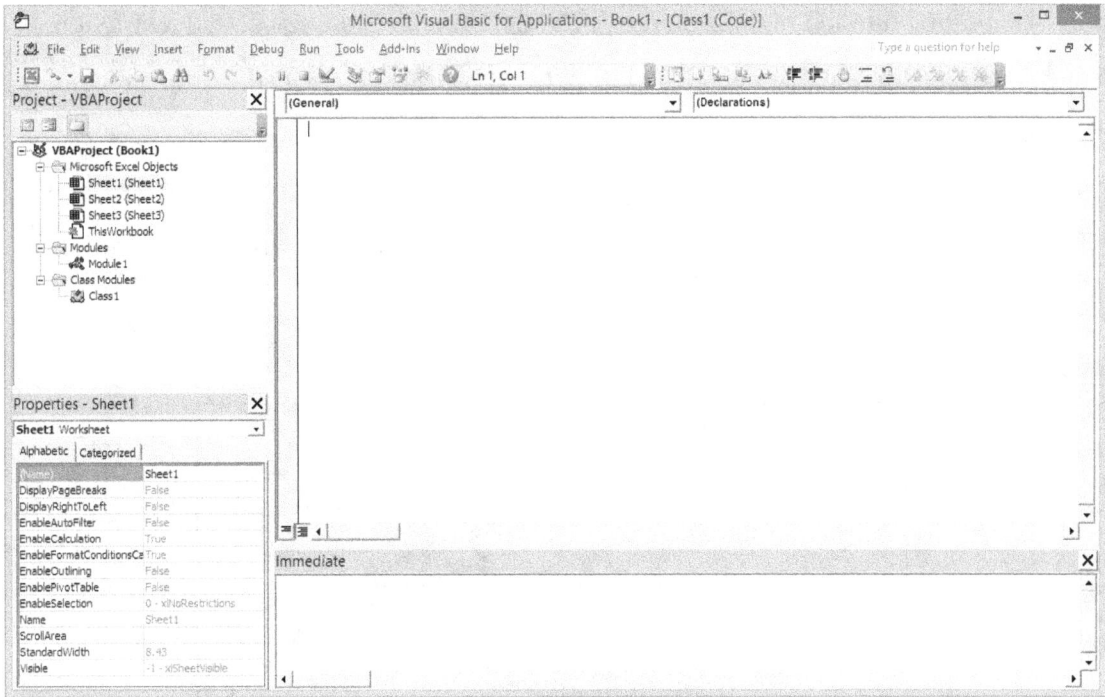

Figure 3.   Screenshot of the VBA IDE contained within all Microsoft Office
products.

B.   RADAR AND JAMMING FUNDAMENTALS

An ideally shaped radar beam produces the three-dimensional (3-D) cone displayed in Figure 4. Concentrated radar energy dissipates and spreads as the wave propagates away from the emitter source. A common practice is to display the radar wave propagation loss by its 3 decibel (dB) loss, which is shown in Figure 5. A more realistic radar pattern is displayed in Figure 6. Design constraints and other natural phenomena cause some radar transmitted energy to be lost through the formation of sidelobes and backlobe. Notice that even if the main beam of the radar is not pointed at the intended target, that same radar target can be identified, albeit at a much shorter range, via the sidelobe energy.

Fortunately for the jamming platform, the sidelobes and backlobe provide additional opportunities to mask the PE from detection. If the AEA jammer's signal is stronger than the PE processed reflected signal in the mainlobe, sidelobes, or backlobe, the radar operator's ability to target the PE with its weapon is severely, if not completely, eliminated.

7

Jamming into the mainlobe and sidelobes does have one additional restriction. To achieve jamming in the main and side lobes, the AEA must be placed within a radar cone, depicted in Figure 4. This restriction is known to AEA operators as elevation and azimuth alignment. Although jamming in the backlobe is permitted, it often requires the AEA asset to be perilously close to the enemy emitter in order to achieve the desired jamming effects.

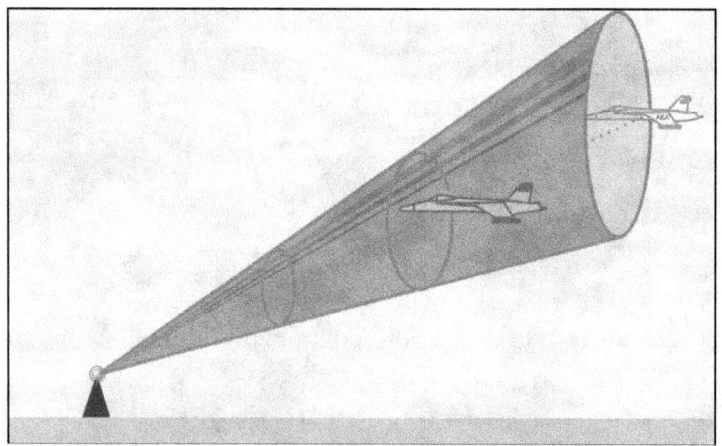

Figure 4.   An ideal 3-D beam produced from a radar. An AEA asset must be within this cone to achieve jamming alignment.

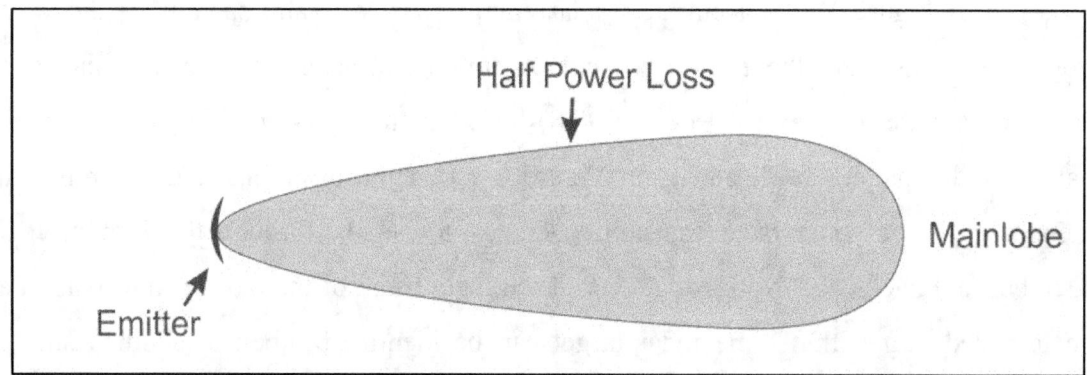

Figure 5.   The typical 3 dB loss propagation pattern used to display radar performance.

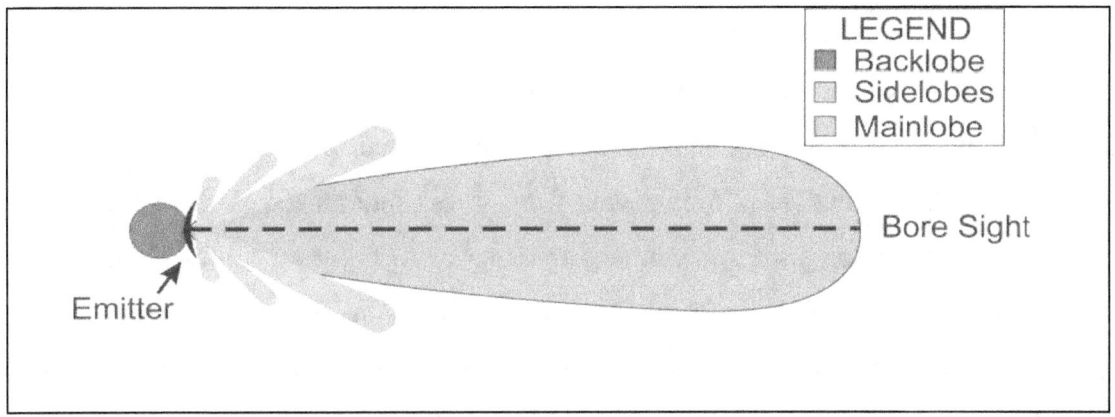

Figure 6.   The complete 3 dB loss propagation pattern of a radar to include
the sidelobes and backlobes transmitted during radar operation.

C.   PROGRAM INPUTS

The four inputs needed to run the EAPPO algorithm are the emitter data, PE strike route, Digital Terrain Elevation Data (DTED), and ALQ-99 or Next Generation Jammer (NGJ) jamming capabilities, which are depicted in Figure 2. First, EAPPO loads emitter data via the EA-6B Tactical Information and Report Management System (ETIRMS) for use in radar range equations defined in the software algorithm section of this chapter. Second, the program requires DTED information to help calculate terrain-impacted radar range rings. Third, the PE strike route is needed to determine the AEA alignment criteria previously discussed. Finally, the developed software requires ALQ-99 effectiveness data to determine the capabilities of the AEA against designated emitters. The ALQ-99 is the jamming system currently employed by the United States onboard the EA-18G Growler.

Three of the four inputs are located on external databases. VBA has the capability of importing the required data directly from the external databases or any other file located on the computer. In addition, VBA user-defined functions are used to provide error checking for the EAPPO algorithms, greatly reducing the potential for data faults located in the external inputs. The methodology for obtaining data from these external databases, leaving the manually entered PE input discussion for Chapter III, is discussed in the remainder of this section.

1. ETIRMS and ALQ-99 Data

Due to the restricted nature of the ALQ-99 capabilities and enemy weapons system emitters, "dummy" notional emitter parameters and locations were created and used in EAPPO simulations. Emitter data were stored into an Excel spreadsheet, with each column containing a specific emitter parameter or ALQ-99 capability. VBA is then used to open a Windows Explorer window to allow the user to select the Excel spreadsheet containing the ALQ-99 and emitter data. VBA searches the opened Excel Spreadsheet headers and extrapolates all the pertinent data. VBA error checking helps ensure all required datum entries are populated.

2. DTED

MIL-PRF-89020B is the standard for DTED information. The standard contains three different resolutions or levels with various classifications. DTED Level 0 contains zero distribution restrictions and can be downloaded from the National Geospatial Intelligence Agency (NGA) website for personal use. The challenge with DTED files is understanding the exact layout of their terrain data. The remaining portion of this section explains the DTED file format and how to extrapolate the terrain data to make the EAPPO map display.

The DTED file format consists of two parts: 1) header and 2) post information [1]. DTED file header information is discussed first.

Every DTED file contains 3428 bytes of header. Contained in the header are five major pieces of information. The five major pieces of information:

1. DTED file Latitude;

2. DTED file Longitude;

3. DTED file Hemisphere location;

4. Number of Latitude Posts;

5. Number of Longitude Posts.

The hexadecimal readout of the first few bytes of information contained in the loaded `42.dt0` file is shown in Figure 7. Bytes 4-16 (`1210000W0420000N`) lets the user know that data contained in this file starts at 42°00'00" N latitude and 121° 00'00" W longitude. Bytes 48-55 (`01210121`) pertain to the number of longitude and latitude data points contained within the DTED file loaded. Given that each DTED file contains 1° of ascending latitude and 1° of deceasing longitude in the northwest hemisphere [1], the data in this particular file is associated with the coordinates 42-43° N latitude and 121-120° W longitude that is further divided 121 times both longitudinally and latitudinally. These results are consistent with the results found in Table 1 derived from MIL-PRF-89020B. The remaining bytes in the header are placeholders and are irrelevant for the intended purpose.

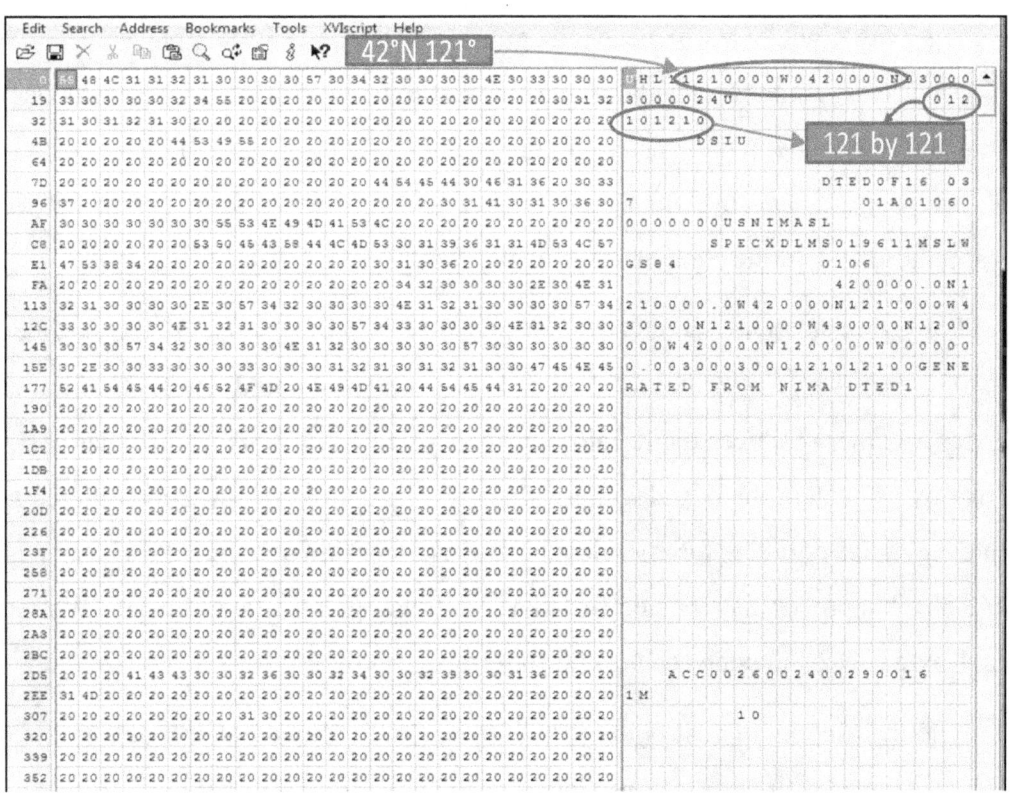

Figure 7.   `42.dto` DTED file header data in hexadecimal used for determining the particulates of the data contained within the opened file.

11

Table 1.   Table containing Level 0 DTED file post information, after [1].

ZONE	LATITUDE DIFFERENCE	MATRIX			
		Latitude Post Difference (seconds)	Number of Latitude Posts	Longitude Post Difference (seconds)	Number of Longitude Posts
I	0° - 50°	30	121	30	121
II	50° - 70°	30	121	60	61
III	70° - 75°	30	121	90	41
IV	75° - 80°	30	121	120	31
V	80° - 90°	30	121	180	21

Actual terrain elevation data does not start until byte 3428 ($D64_{16}$). The 42.dto DTED file hexadecimal readout is shown in Figure 8. Every terrain data point, called a post, starts with eight bytes of header beginning with the hexadecimal value of AA_{16}. The first byte that contains elevation data starts at byte 3436 ($D6C_{16}$) and belongs to the latitude and longitude points listed in the header (42°00 N and 121°00 W). Each individual post is a two-byte unsigned integer in Big Endian format with subsequent posts ascending in latitude along a specific meridian.

For example, bytes 3436 ($D6C_{16}$) and 3437 ($D6D_{16}$) contain the hexadecimal values 05_{16} and $A4_{16}$ for 42°00'00" N and 121° 00'00" W coordinates. Combining the two bytes together produces the terrain elevation value 1444 ($05A4_{16}$) for that post. The next two bytes contain the hexadecimal values 15_{16} and 99_{16}, and when combined makes the integer value of 5529 for the elevation at the coordinates 42°00'30" N and 121° 00'00" W. This process is repeated for all 121 latitude points along the 121°W meridian with a 4-byte checksum added to the end for error checking.

The next meridian post belongs to 120°59'30"W and starts at byte 3682 ($E62_{16}$). Again, AA_{16} denotes the start of post data along a new meridian. Taking into account the remaining data header (7 bytes), we see that the next elevation input starts at bytes 3689 ($E69_{16}$) and 3690 ($E70_{16}$), which contain 05_{16} and BF_{16}. Converting 05_{16} and BF_{16} to a 2-byte integer results in the value of 1471 for the 42°00'00" N and 120°59'30" W coordinate. This process is repeated for the entire length of the file. With the MS Excel

12

built in `freefile`, `open` and `get` function calls, EAPPO is able to read in all the desired DTED posts into a two-dimensional (2-D) array to produce the terrain map.

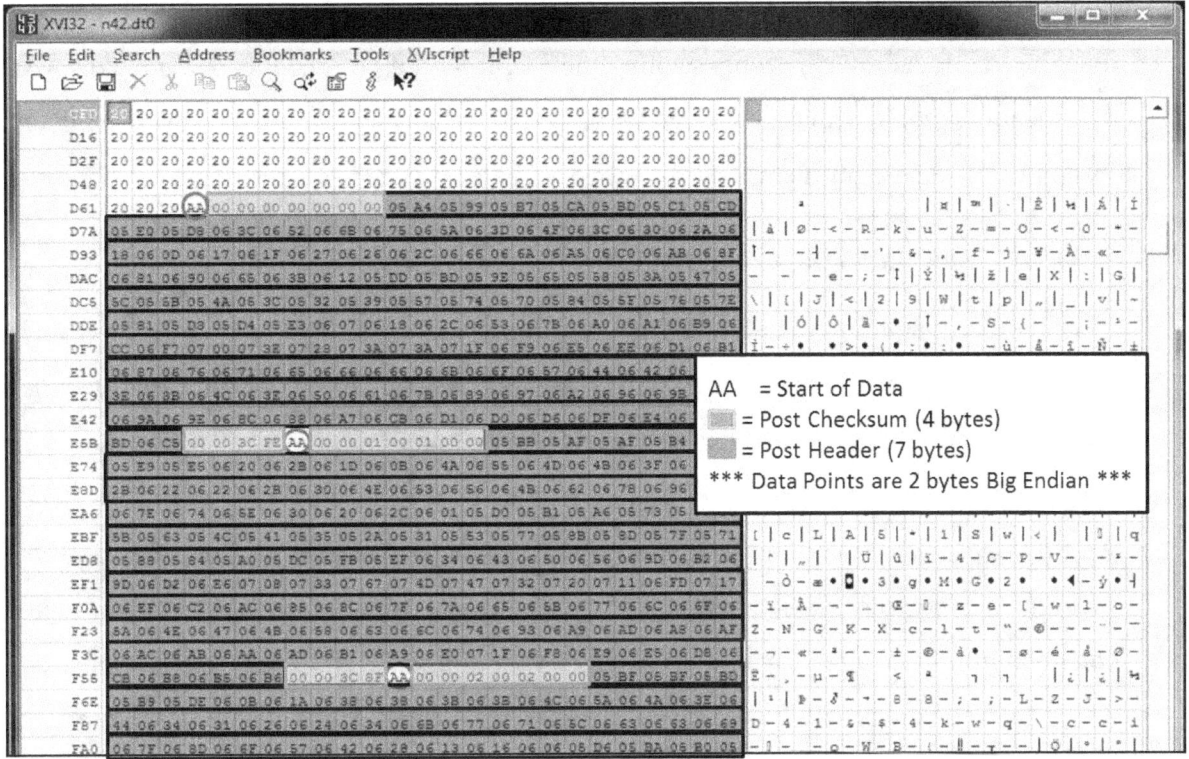

Figure 8.   42.dt0 file post information in hexadecimal used to input terrain
data for the desired grid coordinates.

D.   SOFTWARE ALGORITHMS

With the foundation laid for EAPPO development, the algorithms developed and implemented specifically for this application are now discussed. There were three problems identified with subsequent algorithms developed to meet EAPPO needs. The three problems identified were:

1.   Calculate elevation and azimuth alignment for main and side lobes;

2.   Calculate terrain blockage;

3.   Optimization routine for determining placement of AEA asset.

13

The azimuth and elevation alignment problem is associated with the effective jamming criteria previously mentioned. EAPPO needs to quickly determine the main and side lobe alignment for every emitter along the PE route. The calculate terrain blockage issue addresses radar terrain masking for both the PE and AEA. Obviously, if terrain is blocking the radar energy from reaching the PE, it would not need to be jammed. The optimization problem must provide the best AEA placement in relation to the PE and loaded EOB. These problems and the proposed solution are discussed next.

3. Elevation and Azimuth Alignment for the Mainlobe and Sidelobes

Proper jamming requires both elevation and azimuth alignment. The application software needed an algorithm to quickly determine whether a specific AEA location meets these two alignment criteria at each point along the prescribed PE route. The solution developed proposes dividing the cone shown in Figure 4 into two planes each with an upper and lower bound defined by an equation of a line. Figures 9 and 10 are two-dimensional representations of the radar cones with the red highlighted region conveying the AEA area capable of achieving jamming alignment. Given the upper and lower line equations within a plane, a simple Boolean test is capable of determining whether an AEA location meets the alignment criteria if the AEA is within the line of sight (LOS) with the calculation given by

$$R_{NM} = 1.23 \left(\sqrt{height_{radar}} + \sqrt{height_{AEA}} \right) \tag{1}$$

where R_{NM} is the radar LOS in nautical miles and the $height_{radar}$ and $height_{AEA}$ variables are the radar and AEA height in feet, respectively [2].

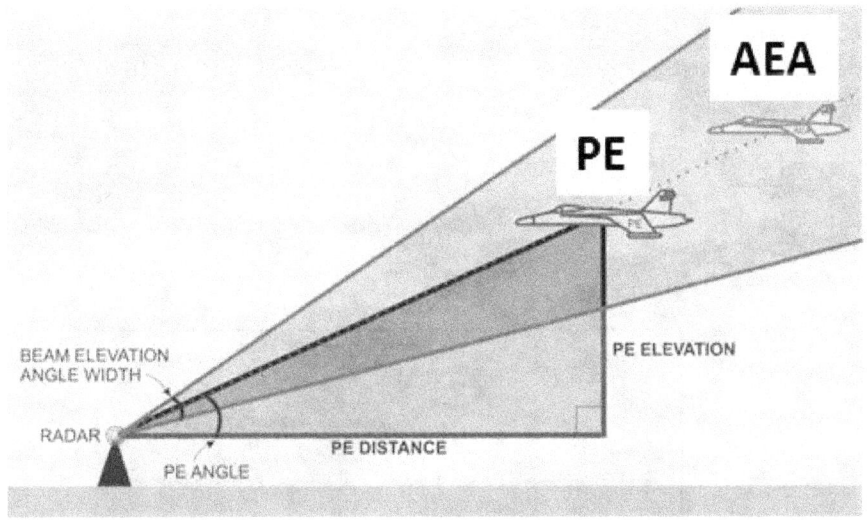

Figure 9.   Two-dimensional elevation plane used to determine radar elevation alignment.

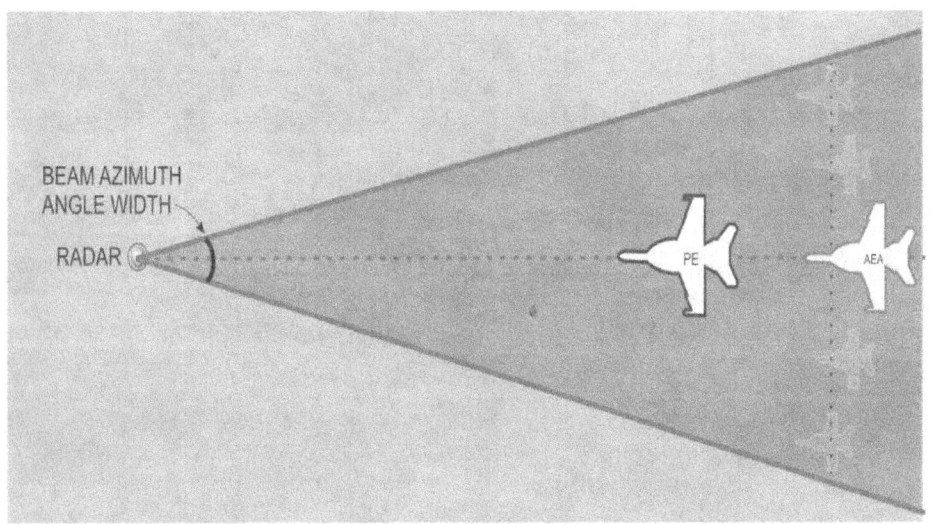

Figure 10.   Two-dimensional plane used for azimuth alignment calculation for AEA asset.

How to properly shade the AEA alignment region is demonstrated in Figure 11. In Figure 11, the $x-y$ plane is divided by the line $f(x,y) = x - 2y + 2$. For any $x-y$ coordinate substituted into $f(x,y) = x - 2y + 2$, there are only three possible outcomes:

1. $f(x,y) > 0$ (point in the positive half-plane);

2. $f(x,y) < 0$ (point in the negative half-plane);

3. $f(x,y)=0$ (point on line).

If the AEA location tested is within the upper and lower bounds in elevation and azimuth, the AEA location is within alignment. Upper and lower line equation derivations for elevation and azimuth, starting with elevation alignment, are discussed in the next two subsections.

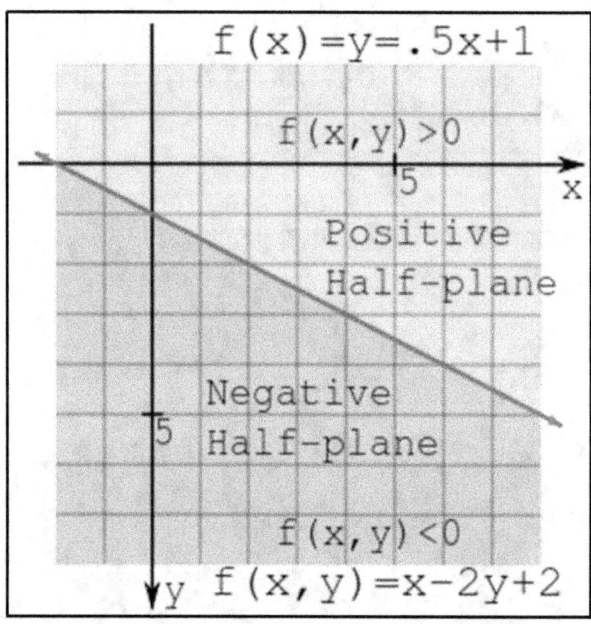

Figure 11.   Positive and negative half-plane division determined by the line $f(x,y)=x-2y+2$ (from [3]).

a.   Elevation Alignment

Figure 12 and the corresponding variable data in Table 2 are used to convey the geometry used to determine elevation alignment. Determining the two line equations consists of four steps. The four steps are:

1.   Calculate PE_{Angle} via

$$PE_{Angle} = \arctan\left(\frac{PE_{Altitude}}{PE_{Distance}}\right) \qquad (2)$$

where PE_{Angle} is the angle between the PE and emitter relative to the earth's surface. $PE_{Altitude}$ and $PE_{Distance}$ are the PE altitude and distance in feet.

16

2. Calculate Upper and Lower Align Angles using

$$Upper\_Align\_Angle = PE_{Angle} + \frac{Emitter\ Beam\ Angle}{2} \tag{3}$$

and

$$Lower\_Align\_Angle = PE_{Angle} + \frac{Emitter\ Beam\ Angle}{2} \tag{4}$$

where *Upper_Align_Angle* and *Lower_Align_Angle* are the maximum and minimum radar beam angles produced by a specific emitter, and *Emitter_Beam_Angle* is the beam angle of the emitter.

3. Calculate *Max_Y* and *Min_Y* which, when coupled with $PE_{Distance}$, produces the two additional points required for the upper and lower elevation alignment line equations:

$$Max\_Y = (PE_{Distance})\tan(Upper\_Align\_Angle) \tag{5}$$

$$Min\_Y = (PE_{Distance})\tan(Upper\_Align\_Angle). \tag{6}$$

4. Calculate upper and lower line equations where x and y are the AEA distance and altitude in feet:

Upper line equation: $\quad 0 = (Max\_Y)x + (PE_{Distance})y \tag{7}$

Lower line equation: $\quad 0 = (Min\_Y)x + (PE_{Distance})y. \tag{8}$

A negative result in Equation (7) and a positive result in Equation (8) quickly determine elevation alignment. The geometry for determining azimuth alignment is discussed in the next section.

Table 2.   List and description of variables required to perform the elevation alignment calculations.

Variable	Formula/Description
$PE_{Altitude}$ (ft.)	Input from user
$PE_{Distance}$ (ft.)	Distance of PE from Emitter
Emitter Elev. Beam Angle (radians)	Emitter Elevation Beam Angle taken from EOB database
PE_{Angle} (radians)	$\arctan\left(\dfrac{PE_{Altitude}}{PE_{Distance}}\right)$
Lower Align Angle (radians)	$PE_{Angle} + \dfrac{Emitter\ Beam\ Angle}{2}$
MIN_Y (ft.)	$(PE_{Distance})\tan(\text{Lower\_Align\_Angle})$
Upper Align Angle (radians)	$PE_{Angle} - \dfrac{Emitter\ Beam\ Angle}{2}$
MAX_Y (ft.)	$(PE_{Distance})\tan(\text{Upper Align Angle})$

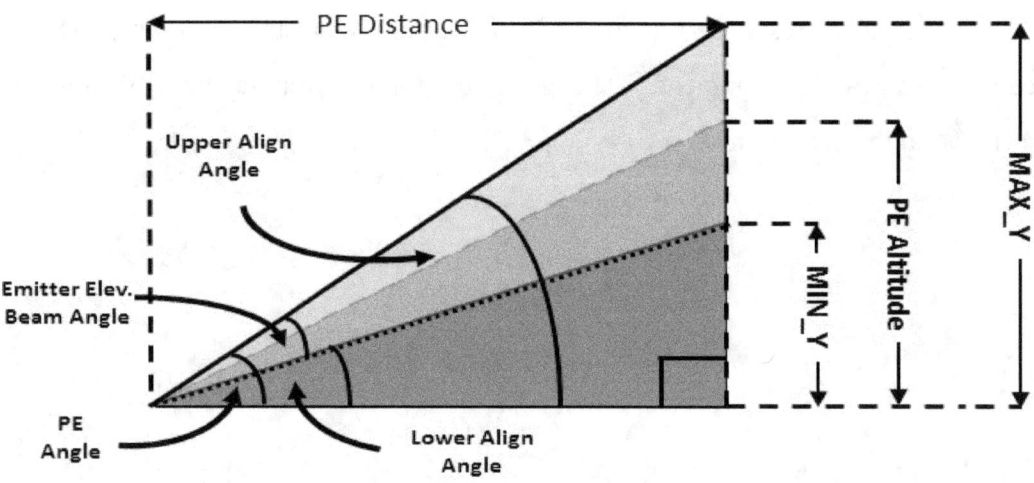

Figure 12.   Geometry used in AEA elevation alignment calculations

18

b. Azimuth Alignment

Figure 13 and the corresponding variable Table 3, are used to convey the geometry used to derive the upper and lower line equations for determining azimuth alignment. It too is a four step process. The four steps are:

1. Calculate *Theta* using

$$Theta = \arctan\left(\frac{Y1 - Y0}{X1 - X0}\right) \tag{9}$$

where *Theta* is defined as the angle between the PE and the emitter. The points $X1, Y1$ and $X0, Y0$ refer to the PE and threat emitter row and column coordinates.

2. Calculate *UpperTheta* and *LowerTheta*,

$$UpperTheta = Theta + \left(\frac{Emitter\_Azimuth\_Beam\_Angle}{2}\right) \tag{10}$$

and

$$LowerTheta = Theta - \left(\frac{Emitter\_Azimuth\_Beam\_Angle}{2}\right), \tag{11}$$

where *UpperTheta* and *LowerTheta* are the upper and lower emitter azimuth beam angles. *Emitter_Azimuth_Beam_Angle* is the emitter's azimuth beam angle.

3. Calculate points $X2$, $Y2$, $X3$, and $Y3$,

$$X2 = (MaxEmitterRange)\cos(LowerTheta), \tag{12}$$
$$Y2 = (MaxEmitterRange)\sin(UpperTheta), \tag{13}$$
$$X3 = (MaxEmitterRange)\cos(LowerTheta), \tag{14}$$

and

$$Y3 = (MaxEmitterRange)\sin(UpperTheta), \tag{15}$$

where *MaxEmitterRange* is the emitters maximum detection range in feet and the points $X2, Y2$ and $X3, Y3$ are used for the upper and lower azimuth alignment equations.

19

4. Derive equations of line for upper and lower azimuth alignment where x and y refer to a row and column value:

$$\text{Upper Line Equation:} \quad 0 = (Y2 - Y0)x - (X2 - X0)y \quad (16)$$

and

$$\text{Lower line equation:} \quad 0 = (Y3 - Y0)x - (X3 - X0)y. \quad (17)$$

Substituting any AEA (x, y) coordinates into Equations (16) and (17) quickly determines azimuth alignment. For example, assume that the values for $X0$, $Y0$, $X2$, $Y2$, $X3$, and $Y3$ are 0, 0, 5, 10, 2, and 1, respectively. Substituting these values into Equations (16) and (17) produces the generalized upper equation $f(x, y) = 5x - 10y$ and the lower equation $f(x, y) = 2x - y$. Consider the AEA (x, y) coordinate to be tested is the point $f(3,3)$. Substituting this value into the upper equation produces a negative result (-15). Likewise, substituting this value into the lower line equation produces a positive result (3). These values tell the software that the grid coordinate $f(3,3)$ is in azimuth alignment. A similar test is conducted to determine elevation alignment criteria using Equations (7) and (8). If the point tested is within the azimuth and elevation upper and lower bounded line equations, the point is in jamming alignment; otherwise, jammer alignment is not achieved, and the tested point does not provide any PE protection. This process is repeated for all possible AEA locations.

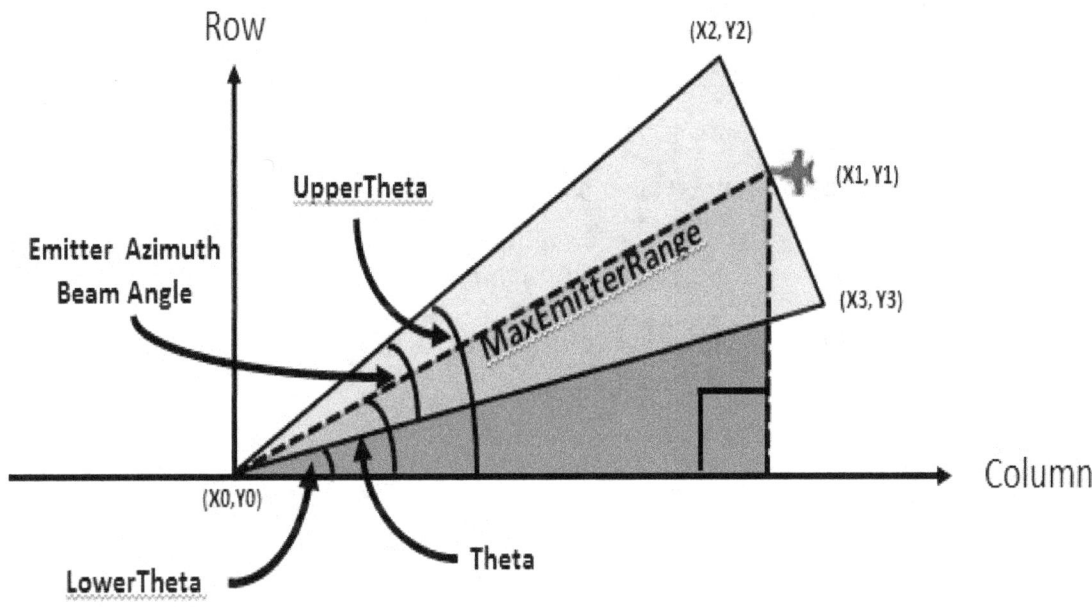

Figure 13.   Geometry used in AEA azimuth alignment calculations.

Table 3.   List and description of variables required to perform the azimuth alignment calculations.

Inputs	
X0	Emitter column
Y0	Emitter row
X1	PE row
Y1	PE column
Angle Calculations	
Theta (radians)	$\arctan\left(\dfrac{Y1-Y0}{X1-X0}\right)$
Half Angle (radians)	$\dfrac{\textit{Emitter Azimuth Beam Angle}}{2}$
Lower Theta (radians)	$\textit{Theta} + \textit{HalfAngle}$
Upper Theta (radians)	$\textit{Theta} - \textit{HalfAngle}$
Outputs	
X2	$(\textit{MaxEmitterRange})\cos(\textit{UpperTheta})$
Y2	$(\textit{MaxEmitterRange})\sin(\textit{UpperTheta})$
X3	$(\textit{MaxEmitterRange})\cos(\textit{LowerTheta})$
Y3	$(\textit{MaxEmitterRange})\sin(\textit{LowerTheta})$

4. Radar Range and Terrain Blocking Calculations

An additional feature designed and developed for EAPPO is the ability to display real-time, updated terrain and jammer impacted range rings. Procedures for adding this feature are discussed in the remaining portions of this section.

a.   *Radar Range Calculation*

The Jammer Techniques Optimization (JATO) radar jamming equation

$$R_{\max} = \left\{ \frac{P_R G_{RT}^2 \sigma \lambda^2 G_m G_i}{(4\pi)^3 (S/N)_{\min} L_{RX} L_{TX} L_{RP} B_R \left[k(T) N_f + \left(\dfrac{\lambda}{4\pi} \right)^2 \displaystyle\sum_{i=1}^{N} \left(\dfrac{P_J G_{JR} G_{RJ}}{R_J^2 B_J} \dfrac{\Delta M}{L_P L_J L_{RX}} \right) \right]} \right\}^{\frac{1}{4}} \tag{18}$$

is used to calculate the jamming impacted emitter range rings [4]. The complete variable description list is found in Table 4. The summation portion of the formula only applies toward stacked beamed radars where the AEA asset achieves jamming alignment in multiple radar beams, creating additive jammer power and reducing the maximum detection range of the radar. If no jamming alignment is achieved, the maximum range is determined using the radar's data located in ETIRMS.

b.   *Terrain Impacted Range Rings*

How to calculate the radar terrain and jamming impacted range ring is discussed in this section. We start by dividing the PE altitude by its grid distance to produce a constant elevation change per pixel from the emitter to the PE. Next, we draw a concentric circle around a specific threat emitter using the well-known Bresenham [5] circle algorithm to return the circle endpoints along a given radius. With the circle endpoints calculated, a line is drawn from the threat emitter to each of the endpoints using the Bresenham line algorithm.

Table 4.   List and descriptions of variables used in JATO range equation.

NUMERATOR	
P_R	Transmitter peak power (kW)
G_{RT}	Transmitter antenna gain (dBi)
σ	Radar cross section of PE (m^2)
λ	Transmitter wavelength (m)
G_m	Transmitter compression gain (dB)
G_i	Transmitter integration gain (dB)
DENOMINATOR	
S/N_{min}	Minimum signal to noise ratio required for PE detection (dB)
L_{RX}	Transmitter hardware losses such as cable and radome losses (dB)
L_{RP}	Miscellaneous radar processing losses (dB)
B_R	Receiver bandwidth (megahertz)
k	Boltzmann's constant $\left(1.3806488 \cdot 10^{-23} \dfrac{m^2 kg}{s^2 K}\right)$
T	Temperature (290 K)
N_f	Receiver noise figure (dB)
λ	Transmitter wavelength (m)
P_J	Jammer peak power (W)
G_{JR}	Jammer receiver antenna gain (dBi)
G_{RJ}	Jammer receiver gain (dB)
ΔM	Jammer technique modulation gain (dB)
R_J	Jammer range (nmi)
B_J	Jammer bandwidth (MHz)
L_P	Polarization mismatch loss (dB)
L_J	Miscellaneous jammer loss (dB)
L_{RX}	Receiver processing loss (dB)
$\sum_{i=1}^{N}$	Used for fixed stacked radar beams where AEA is successful in jamming in multiple aligned beams. N is number of stacked beams.

At any time, if the pixel terrain value is greater than the incremented elevation, terrain is blocking the radar LOS to the PE and a new circle endpoint is produced. Otherwise, the previous circle endpoint is maintained. Repeating this process for all the circle's endpoints, the algorithm again uses the Bresenham line algorithm to connect the calculated endpoints together to produce the updated jamming and terrain impacted range rings. A screenshot of the terrain impacted range rings is depicted in Figure 14.

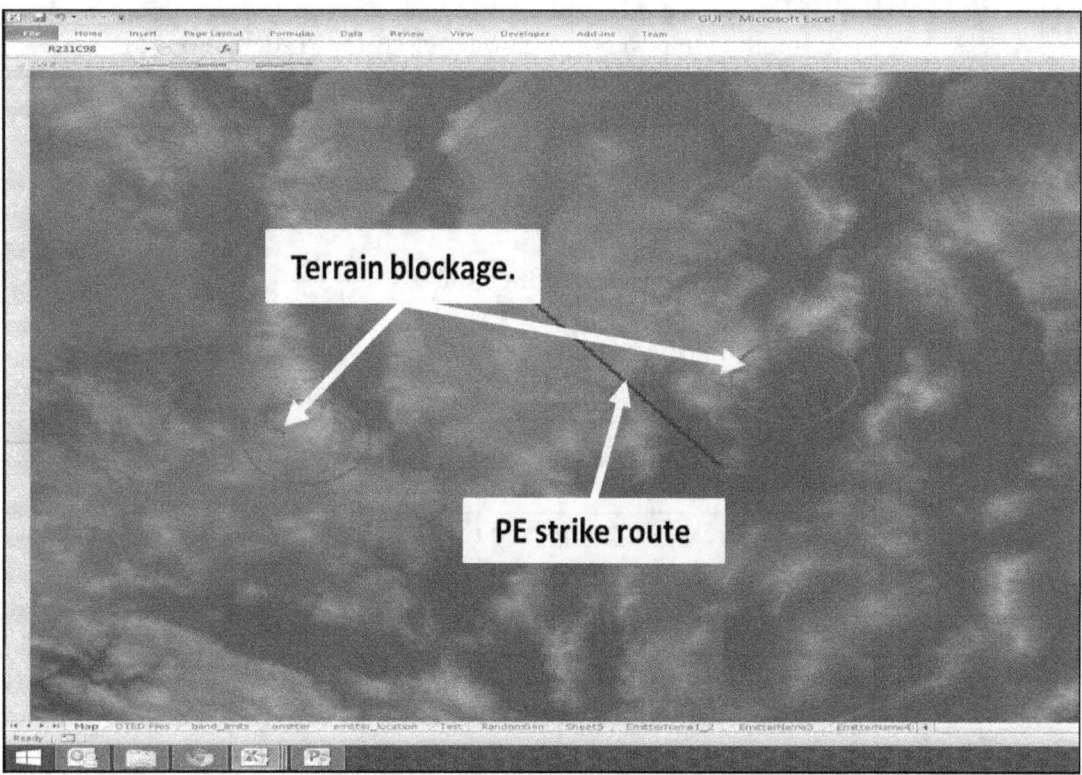

Figure 14. Screenshot displaying terrain impacted range rings.

5. Optimization Algorithm

The next algorithm discussed in this thesis is the optimization algorithm developed for determining the optimal placement of the AEA asset relative to the desired PE route. Two different approaches were developed and attempted. The first approach was to use linear programming coupled with a branch-and-bound additive algorithm outlined in [6]. Linear programming is a method for maximizing or minimizing a function, called the objective function, using only linear functions whose variables are subject to constraints. The EAPPO maximization objective function is defined as

$$\max_X \sum_{i,j,k} Array_{i,j,k} X_{i,j,k} \tag{19}$$

where X is the decision variable, $Array_{i,j,k}$ is a 3D jamming values array, i equals the number of PE strike route points, and j,k are the 2-D row and column jamming effectiveness matrix values produced for a particular strike route point. Linear programming constraints are defined by

$$\sum_{i,j,k} X_{i,j,k} = 1 \ \forall \ i \tag{20}$$

and

$$
\begin{aligned}
X_{i,j,k} \leq [X_{i-1,j-1,k} + X_{x-1,j+1,k} + X_{i-1,j,k} + X_{i-1,j,k+1} + X_{i-1,j,k-1} \\
+ X_{i-1,j+1,k+1} + X_{i-1,j-1,k+1} + X_{i-1,j-1,k-1} + X_{i-1,j+1,k-1}], \ \forall \ i \geq 2, j, k,
\end{aligned}
\tag{21}
$$

where the constraint in Equation (20) pertains to the fact that the AEA aircraft can only be at one designated point in the map at a time, and the constraint in Equation (21) means that the AEA can only proceed to a maximum of one grid coordinate difference away from its current $X_{i,j,k}$ location.

The drawback of using the first method is its inability to concurrently determine the maximum jamming values for multiple $x-y$ grid coordinates. Every possible AEA location along $Array_{1,j,k}$ has to be computed, potentially duplicating central processing unit (CPU) work.

This drawback led to the development and implementation of a dynamic programming approach. The algorithm produced contains four steps listed below. The four steps are:

1.   Calculate 2-D jamming array for all radar threats for every point along PE strike route to populate $Array_{i,j,k}$;

2.   For all values of i, use

$$JarArray_{i+1,j,k} = Array_{i+1,j,k} + max \begin{pmatrix} Array_{i,j-1,k}, Array_{i,j,k}, Array_{i,j+1,k}, \\ Array_{i,j,k-1}, Array_{i,j+1,k-1}, Array_{i,j-1,k-1}, \\ Array_{i,j+1,k+1}, Array_{i,j-1,k+1}, Array_{i,j,k+1} \end{pmatrix} \forall i \geq 1 \quad (22)$$

to populate a new additive jamming array called $JarArray_{i,j,k}$.

3. Calculate the AEA optimized route using

$$AEA\_Route_{i,j,k} = \left[max\left(JarArray_{i-1,j,k} \right) \right.$$
$$+ max \begin{pmatrix} JarArray_{i,j-1,k}, JarArray_{i,j,k}, JarArray_{i,j+1,k}, \\ JarArray_{i,j,k-1}, JarArray_{i,j+1,k-1}, JarArray_{i,j-1,k-1}, \\ JarArray_{i,j+1,k+1}, JarArray_{i,j-1,k+1}, JarArray_{i,j,k+1} \end{pmatrix} \right], \forall i \geq 2 \quad (23)$$

where the algorithm selects the highest jamming values contained in $JarArray$ for all $i \geq 2$.

4. Designate a value for each point along the AEA route to be later colored using MS Excel conditional formatting. EAPPO AEA route was given a value of two.

A screenshot shown in Figure 15 is an example of the optimization algorithm. The data in the left column (columns G-K) refer to jamming effectiveness $Array_{i,j,k}$ where $i, j,$ and k equal five. The data in the right column (columns M-Q) refer to $JarArray_{i,j,k}$. Start by copying the bottom block of data in $Array_{bottom,j,k}$ to $JarArray_{bottom,j,k}$. To find the maximum jamming value reachable in cell O21 (purple circle), add cell I21 (red circle = 6) to the maximum value contained in cells N26, N27, N28, O26, O27, O28, P26, P27, and P28 (blue square in bottom right data block = 8). This produces the result 14 (6+8) into cell O21. This process is repeated for all remaining values of i.

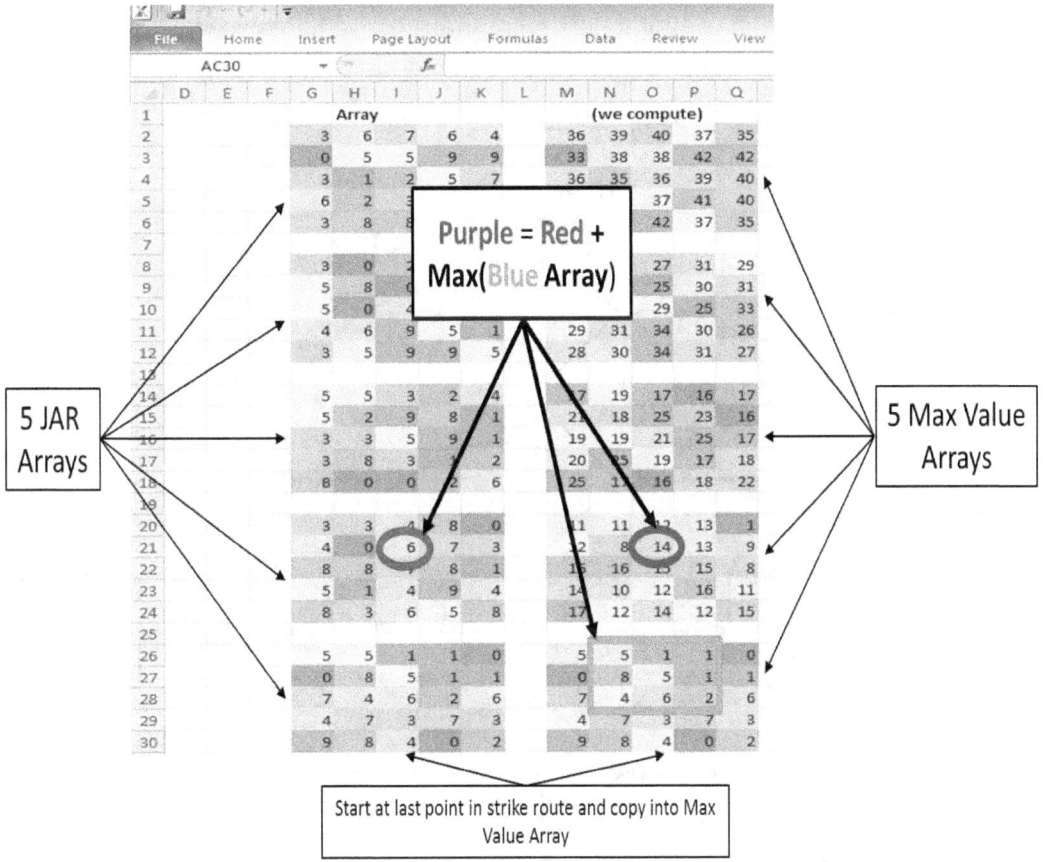

Figure 15. Screenshot showing EAPPO's optimization algorithm using dynamic programming.

E. AEA OPTIMIZATION ALGORITHM

The solutions to the three problems discussed in previous section produce the AEA optimization algorithm process flowchart depicted in Figure 16. The process starts with an AEA location with an unknown jamming alignment. The first calculation is to determine if the AEA location has achieved emitter elevation alignment. The algorithm then branches to either a mainlobe azimuth calculation or sidelobes elevation alignment calculation.

If the AEA location achieves mainlobe elevation alignment, the next calculation tests for mainlobe azimuth alignment. If the AEA location produces both mainlobe elevation and azimuth alignment, the jamming effectiveness array is incremented by three; else the process proceeds to the sidelobes azimuth alignment calculation. The more restrictive mainlobe elevation alignment criterion automatically places the AEA within sidelobes elevation alignment, bypassing the sidelobes elevation alignment calculation.

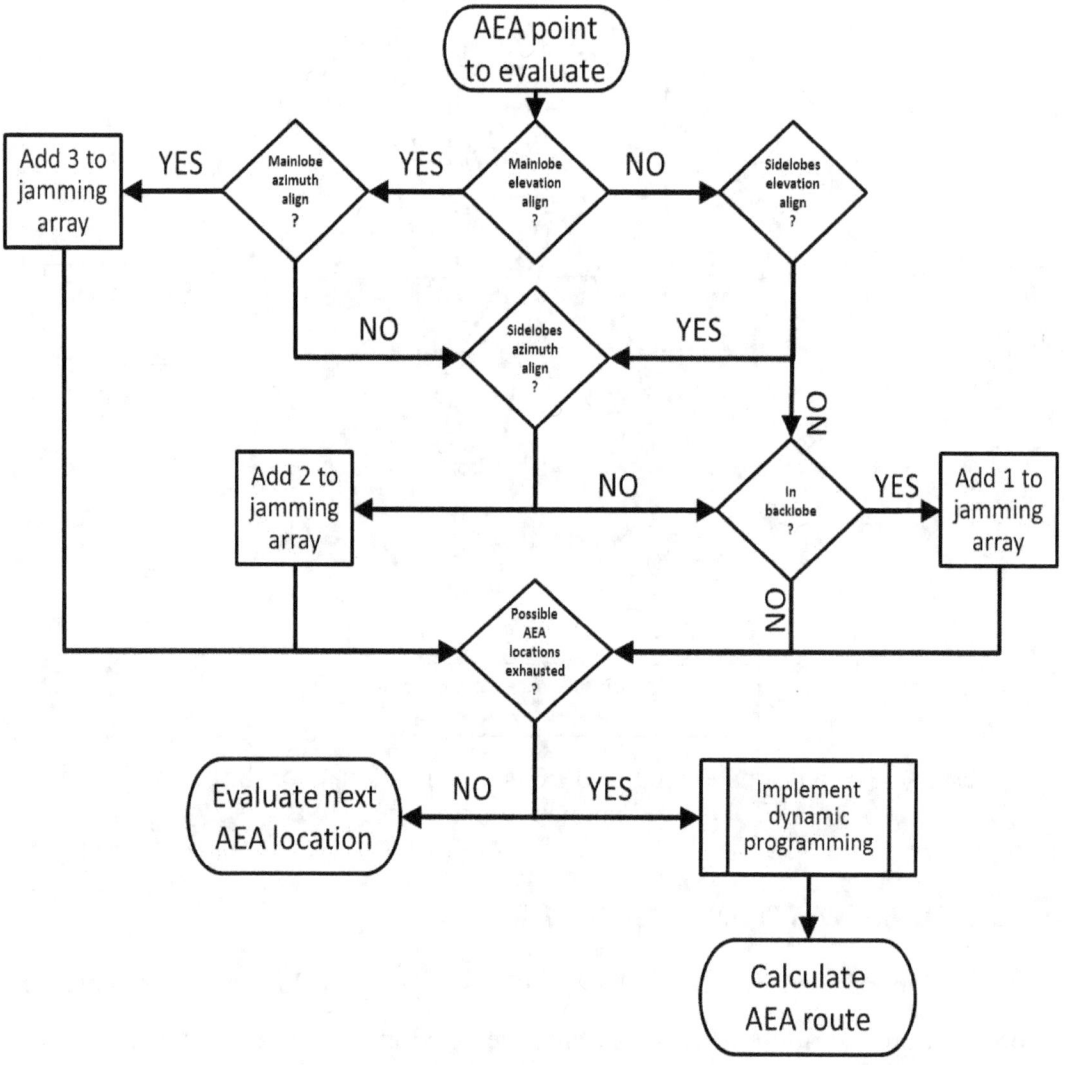

Figure 16.   AEA placement optimization flowchart depicting the steps to determine optimal AEA location for a particular PE strike route and EOB.

If the initial test for mainlobe elevation alignment proves negative, a repeat calculation is done to determine sidelobes elevation alignment, producing another branch in the algorithm process. Similar to the mainlobe calculation, if the AEA location achieves sidelobes elevation alignment, then the next step is to check for sidelobes azimuth alignment. A positive sidelobes azimuth alignment calculation increments the jamming effectiveness array by two. A negative result forces the algorithm to check for backlobe alignment.

If the tests for sidelobes elevation alignment or sidelobes azimuth alignment prove negative, the next calculation preformed is to determine if the AEA is within the emitter backlobe alignment. Again, the algorithm branches on the result. If the AEA location is within the emitter backlobe, the jamming effectiveness array is incremented by one; otherwise, AEA location evaluated produces zero jamming, and the jamming effectiveness array is not incremented. This process is repeated for all emitters and all possible AEA locations. Once the possible AEA location values are exhausted, the optimized AEA location and quantifiable jamming effectiveness outputs are produced via dynamic programming.

F.   MOVING MAP IN MS EXCEL

All the previous steps and algorithms laid the groundwork for the culminating EAPPO output, a moving map in MS Excel. The moving map built contains terrain data in grayscale, PE and AEA route overlays, threat emitter objects, terrain and jamming impacted range rings, and, finally, animation to convey the updated radar threats along the PE and AEA routes. The procedures for implementing these five features in MS Excel are discussed in the remaining portions of this section.

1.   Creating a Grayscale Map

Once the DTED information has been read in and is contained in a 2-D array, the terrain data must be displayed in an Excel worksheet for use by the operator. There are many approaches to accomplish this task, each with varying degrees of success. Research proved the fastest way to transport and color data from VBA to an Excel worksheet is to first transfer the entire 2-D array to the Excel worksheet using the worksheet range object and then use Excel's conditional formatting feature to color the individual cells contained in the worksheet [7].

Knowing the algorithm would have additional overlays on top of the terrain map, VBA was used to quantize the DTED integer values into 256 different grayscale values, and then 1000 was added to that value to ensure that all the terrain values were between 1000 and 1256. The 2-D grayscale quantized terrain array *colorMap* is produced from using

$$colorMap_{row,column} = int\left(\frac{DTEDArray_{row,column}}{maxDTEDValue}\right)256 + 100 \qquad (24)$$

where $DTEDArray_{row,column}$ the 2-D raw DTED array, $maxDTEDValue$ is the maximum integer value contained in $DTEDArray$, and *int* is a VBA function that returns a 2-byte signed integer value regardless of the calculation performed.

Once the 2-D array is quantized, it can be transferred to the desire worksheet. The data contained in the worksheet is then colored using conditional formatting to produce the grayscale map shown in Figure 17.

Figure 17.   DTED grayscale map produce by conditional formatting.

2. Adding PE and AEA Routes

Another visual aid desired by the operator and developed by the thesis application is the PE and AEA route overlays. The AEA route was developed in Step 5 of the optimization algorithm. The AEA route point assigned value is '2'. Conditional formatting is then used to color all worksheet cells with the value '2' the color green. To display the PE route, the Bresenham Line algorithm is used to connect the user inputted waypoints and give the returned values a value of '1.' Conditional formatting then colors the strike route points blue.

3. Add Emitter Range Rings

To add the emitter range rings along the route, we apply the Radar Range and Terrain Blocking Calculations algorithms previously discussed. For each threat emitter, we determine the range endpoints and assign them a value of '3.' Conditional formatting is applied to color the endpoints red. The complete list of applied conditional formatting is shown in Figure 18.

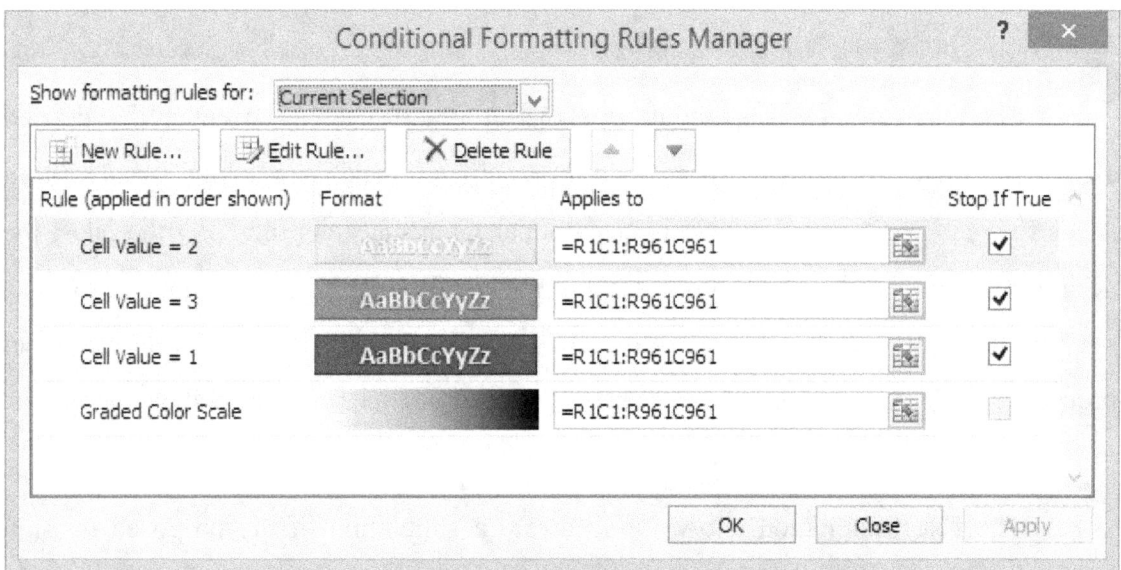

Figure 18.   Screenshot of applied conditional formatting used to color worksheet.

4. Adding Objects to Represent Emitter Locations and Air Assets

The final overlays developed for use in the EAPPO map are the emitter location, AEA location, and PE location visual aids. For the emitter location visual aid, VBA is used to add an Excel rectangular shape object to the map at the desired emitter

31

coordinates. Adding unique emitter text to the created rectangular object quickly allows the operator to delineate between the different emitter objects on the map.

For the PE and AEA visual aids, airplane images are added to the map worksheet, matching their color with their respective route. EAPPO then used VBA to control the airplane image rotation and location as the airplane proceeds along its intended flight path. The aforementioned features allow real-time jamming analysis and tremendous situation awareness for aircraft during bombing missions.

5. Excel Animation

The final software feature developed in this application is animation. Animation greatly enhances the visualization effects of the preceding algorithms. The software achieves animation by using the VBA `Application.OnTime` method. The `Application.OnTime` method has 4 inputs: 1) `Earliest Time`, 2) `Procedure`, 3) `Latest Time`, and 4) `Schedule` [8].

The `Earliest Time` input tells the program when to execute the desired algorithm. The `Procedure` input tells the computer which procedure the algorithm needs to run. The `Latest Time` is an optional input that tells the CPU the latest the desired program listed in the Procedure can run. The final input called `Schedule` is also optional and tells the CPU whether to start a new procedure or clear a previously set procedure [8]. The splashscreen shown in Figure 19 was created using the `Application.OnTime` method.

The Excel animation allows us to create a simulation of the proposed mission taking into account the location of the AEA, PE, and EOB to display jamming and terrain impacted threat range rings along the prescribed strike route. The EAPPO results are conveyed in Chapter III of this thesis.

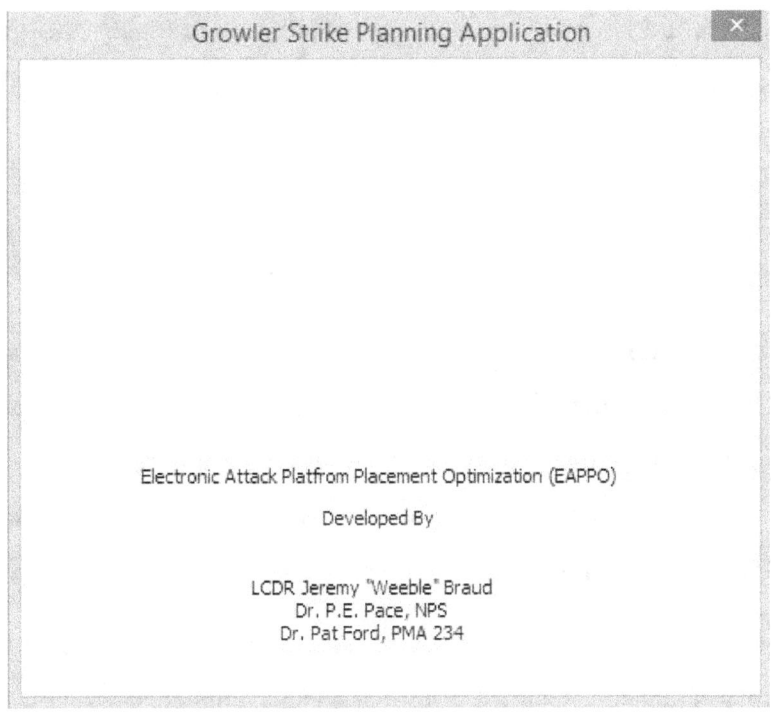

Figure 19. Splashscreen created for jamming optimization algorithm
application using MS Excel's `Applicatin.OnTime` method.

G. ADDITIONAL   CAPABILITIES   DEVELOPED   BUT   NOT IMPLEMENTED

There were two capabilities investigated but not implemented in the final software produced. The two capabilities investigated were 1) parallel processing and 2) client-server application using VBA. The purpose and feasibilities of these two capabilities are discussed the remaining sections in this chapter.

1. Parallel Processing in VBA

A major drawback in using VBA programming is that VBA is limited to serial program execution. VBA has zero libraries for parallel programming or multithreading; however, VBA does allow for external libraries to be used for parallel computations on the Graphical Processing Unit (GPU). The GPU is a relative new piece computer hardware initially used for high speed graphics in the gaming community. The GPU's parallel processing capability can be used to augment the serial processing used in VBA.

Successful experiments validated the possibility of using the GPU from MS Excel. The steps taken to accomplish this task are outlined in the Appendix. Real-time AEA optimization flight calculations must use the GPU to improve the algorithms performance.

2. Client-Server Using Two Different Excel Application

The second feature researched but not implemented in the final product was the feasibility of setting up a Client-Server type application using only pre-approved software products. Real-time jamming effectiveness calculations require updated AEA, PE, and emitter locations. Excel or any other commercial software employed needs to be able to receive the updated information.

In earlier versions of Microsoft Office, there was an ability to use `TcpClient` class to set up a Transport Control Protocol (TCP) connection. Unfortunately, this capability is not available in more modern MS Office suites such as MS Office 2010. Instead, setting up a TCP socket requires using the Winsock Application Program Interface (API) libraries built into Window. Converting Winsock API reference functions displayed in Figure 20 to applicable VBA code, we conducted successful experiments by transmitting and receiving data using two Excel applications on separate workstations over a WiFi communication link.

The benefit of such an approach is the unique ability to create ad hoc networks using non-compliable code. The AEA mission computer can be configured to send one-way communication to the tablet, providing the necessary software inputs needed to run the previously discussed algorithms.

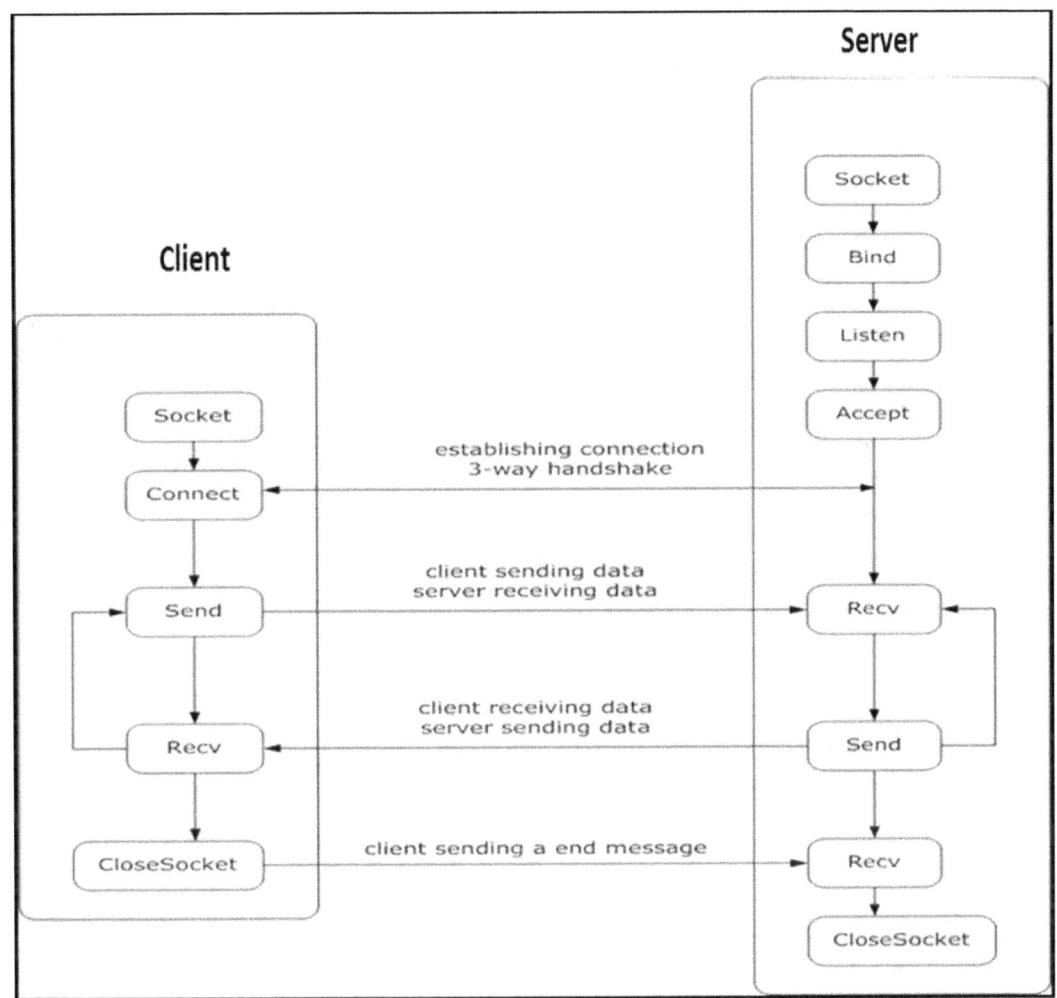

Figure 20.   WINSOCK API Functions needed to use TCP via VBA, from [9].

THIS PAGE INTENTIONALLY LEFT BLANK

III. PROGRAM FLOW AND JAMMING WIZARD USERFORM

The complete program flowchart can be found in Figure 21, where the rows delineate between the inputs, AEA placement optimization algorithm, and outputs shown in Figure 2. A simple wizard was created using a userform in VBA to give EAPPO a modern look and feel for the operator. The developed wizard called Jamming Wizard contains five steps to ensure the software receives the required inputs outlined in Figure 2. The five steps are:

1.   PE and JX emitter data entry;

2.   Loading the enemy order of battle;

3.   Loading DTED files;

4.   Selecting emitters to be jammed;

5.   Entering PE waypoints.

The functionality of the wizard using screenshots to display EAPPO's user interface are discussed in the remaining sections of this chapter.

A.   PE AND JX DATA

Figure 22 is the first page of the Jamming Wizard userform. It has three user required inputs. `Select the PE` textbox is used in Equation (18) to populate the PE radar cross-section (σ) variable. `Enter PE Altitude in ft` and the `Enter Jammer Altitude in ft` textboxes are used to determine AEA elevation alignment outlined in Chapter II. Once the three textboxes are populated, the user selects the `next` button to proceed to step 2 of the Jamming Wizard.

B.   ENEMY ORDER OF BATTLE (EOB)

The next step in the Jamming Wizard is to have the user load the desired EOB shown in Figure 23. An event is triggered when the MS userform `Load Emitter Data` control button is clicked. The event opens the Windows Explorer window shown in Figure 24.

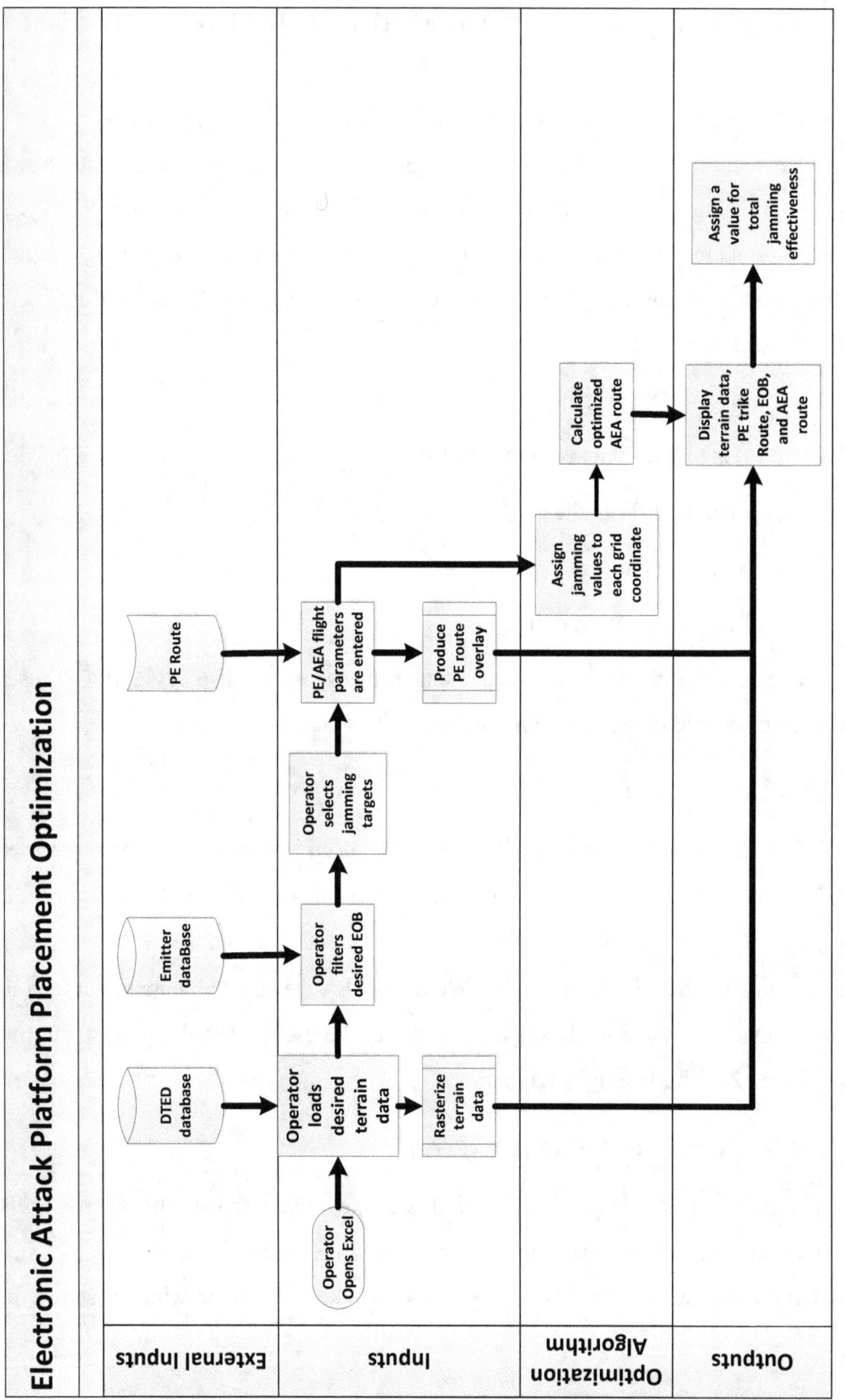

Figure 21. EAPPO program flowchart depicting the external inputs and data processing.

The user then selects the appropriate emitter Excel file containing the emitter and jammer parameters used in Equation (18). Once selected, VBA code is used to populate VBA class objects with the required data. Clicking the `Next>>` command button takes the operator to step 3 of the Jamming Wizard.

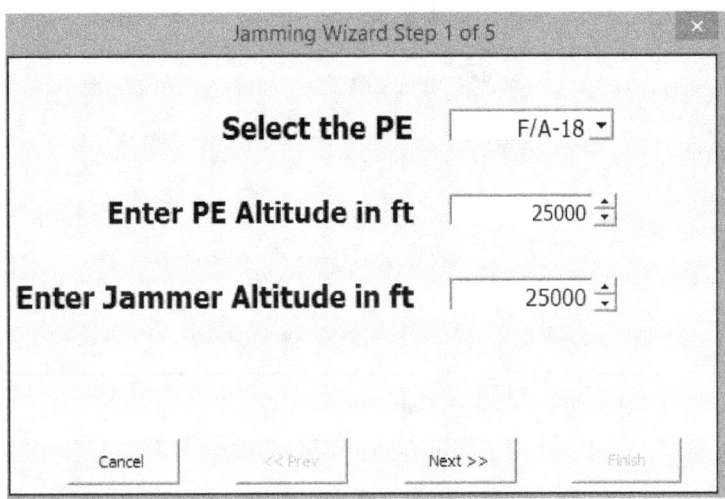

Figure 22.   PE and JX data page of Jamming Wizard userform used to populate PE's radar cross section, PE altitude, and AEA altitude.

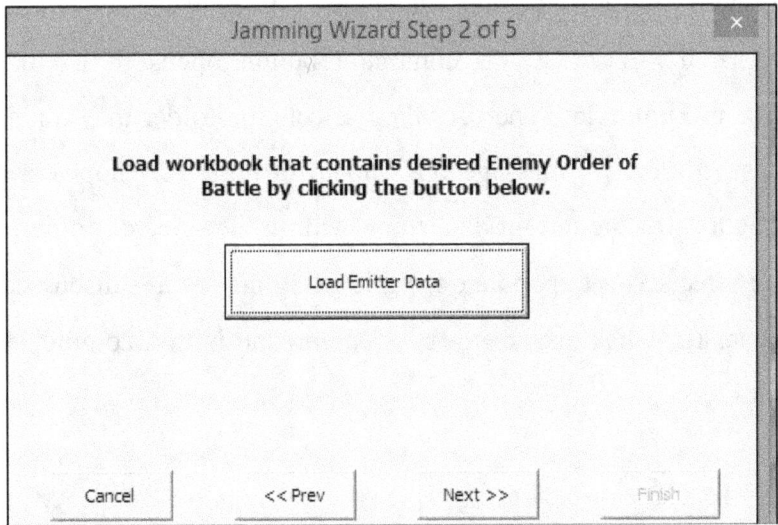

Figure 23.   Load Emitter Page of Jamming Wizard userform used to select EOB file.

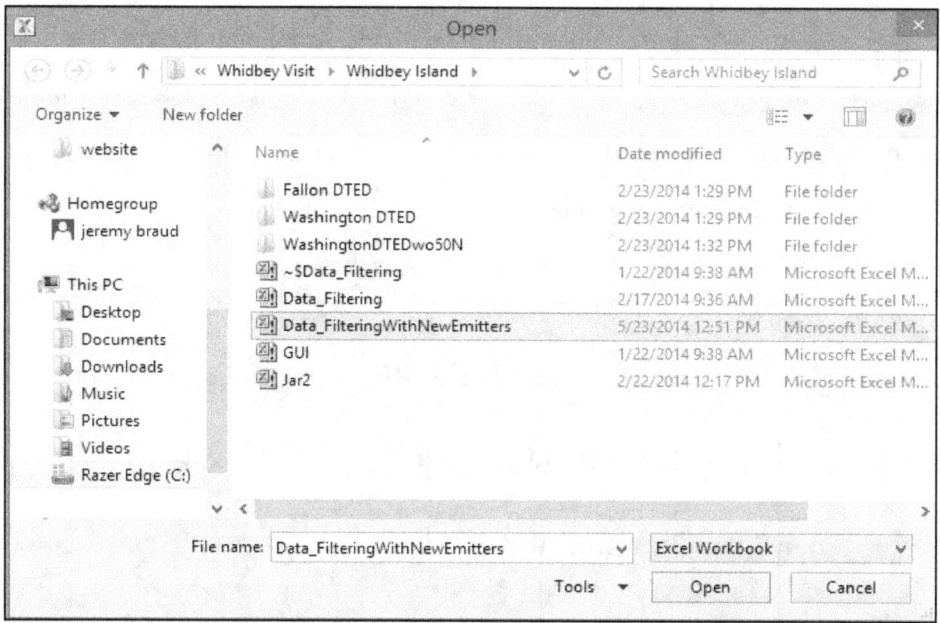

Figure 24.   Window Explorer Tab Opened from Jamming Wizard userform
used to populate variables in JATO range equation.

C.   LOAD DTED

The next step in the Jamming Wizard, which entails loading the DTED files used for map coloring and terrain blocking calculations, is shown in Figure 25. Similar to loading the EOB, the `Load DTED` command button opens the Windows Explorer window pictured in Figure 26. The user then selects the folder that contains the DTED files for the desired area. A message box shown in Figure 27 appears, displaying the latitude and longitude of the terrain data found within the selected folder. If the data is correct, the user selects `Yes` to populate the grid using procedures discussed in the DTED section of Chapter II. Clicking the `Next >>` command button completes Step 3 of the Jamming Wizard.

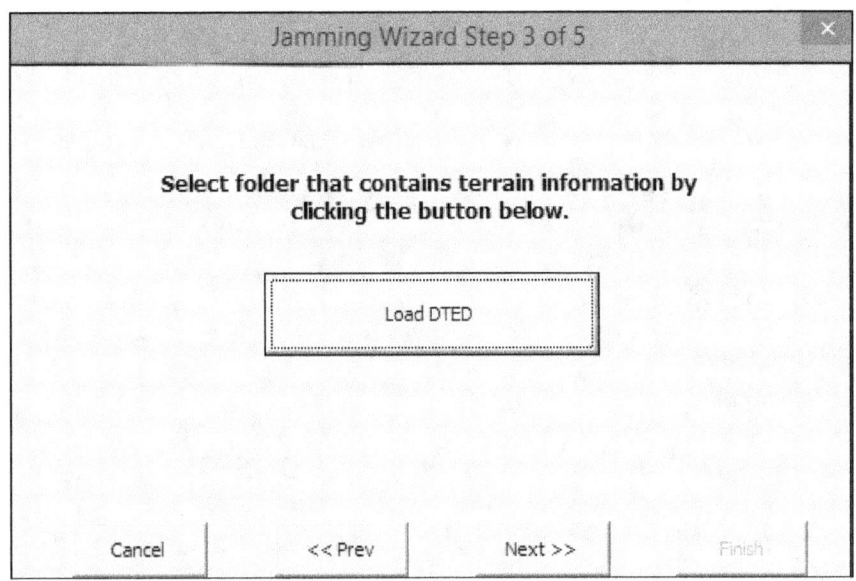

Figure 25.   Load DTED page of Jamming Wizard userform used to load terrain data.

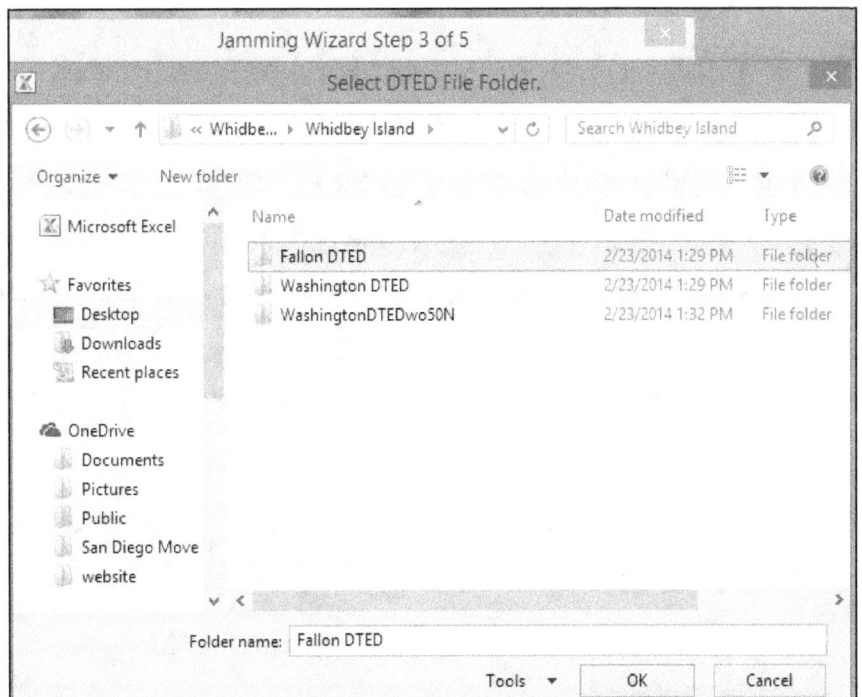

Figure 26.   Window Explorer tab opened from Jamming Wizard userform asking the user to select DTED folder.

41

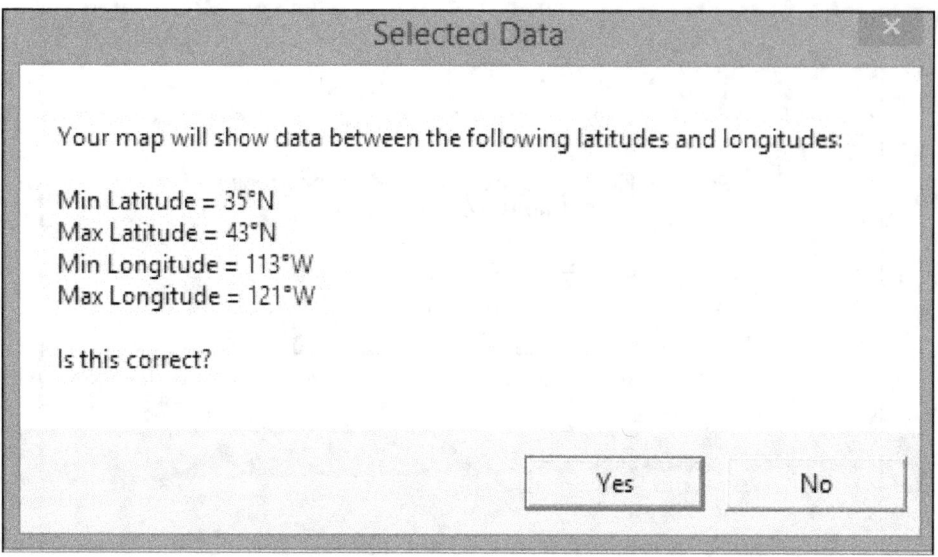

Figure 27.   Message box containing latitude and longitude of DTED files
contained within the user selected folder.

D.   SELECT EMITTERS TO BE JAMMED

In Step 4 of the Jamming Wizard, the user selects the emitters they want to display and target during the specific mission. The `Available Emitters` listbox was populated from the EOB workbook loaded in Step 2 of the Jamming Wizard. The operator then uses the `Add Emitter>>` command button to populate the `Emitters to be Jammed` listbox. All emitters contained in the `Emitters to be Jammed` listbox are used to determine the optimal AEA location. Figure 28 is the screenshot showing the operators desire to jam and plot the dummy emitter **EWEMIT01** for this mission.

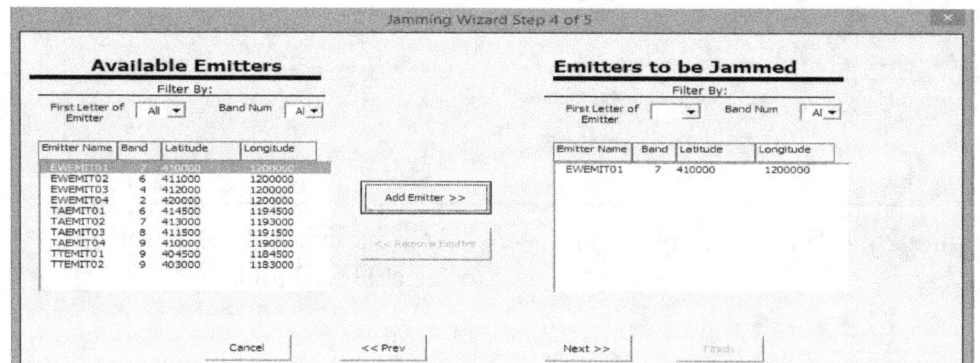

Figure 28.   Emitters to be jammed page of Jamming Wizard to allow user to
select EOB for desired mission.

42

E.   ENTER PE STRIKE ROUTE

The Jamming Wizard concludes with the operator entering the PE strike route. Once the waypoints are entered, latitude and longitude coordinates are transformed to Excel grid (row and column) coordinates. After that, the Bresenham line algorithm is used to connect the waypoints, giving EAPPO the required PE path needed for the jammer alignment algorithms discussed in "Optimization Algorithm" section contained Chapter II. A screenshot of this step in the Jamming Wizard is shown in Figure 29.

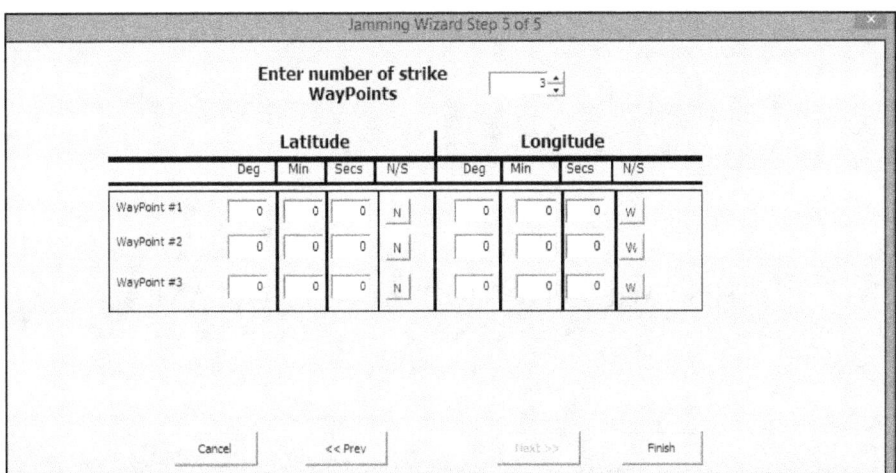

Figure 29.   Waypoint entry page of the Jamming Wizard used to enter PE waypoints.

THIS PAGE INTENTIONALLY LEFT BLANK

IV.   MODEL FORMULATION AND SIMULATION RESULTS

A.   MODEL FORMULATION

The complete list of inputs and dummy emitter parameters used for the simulation can be found in Table 5. DTED data for Naval Air Station (NAS) Fallon was loaded in hopes of testing the full functionality of the software at the NAS Fallon electronic warfare range. The results of EAPPO simulation using the given parameters found in Tables 5 and 6 are discussed in the remaining sections of this chapter.

Table 5.   The PE parameters and waypoints used for EAPPO simulation.

INPUT	VALUE	
PE radar cross section look up	2 m^2	
PE altitude	25000 ft.	
AEA altitude	25000 ft.	
PE Waypoints		
Waypoint number	Latitude	Longitude
Waypoint #1	42° 00 00 N	120° 45 00 W
Waypoint #2	41° 10 00 N	120° 10 00 W

Table 6. EOB and jammer performance parameters used for the EAPPO simulation.

EOB	
Simulated Emitter Name	**Emitter Location**
EWEMIT01	N 41° 00.00 W 121° 00.00
EWEMIT01 Simulated Parameters	
Peak power	1200 W
Transmitter antenna gain	41 dB
Receiver antenna gain	41 dBi
Center frequency	2900 MHz
Compression gain	0 dB
Integration gain	6 dB
Detection signal to noise ratio	13 dB
Receiver losses	2 dB
Transmitter losses	2 dB
Processing losses	1 dB
IF bandwidth	0.70 MHz
Noise figure	4.50 dB
Jammer Capabilities Against EWEMIT01	
Jammer peak power	1500 W
Jammer antenna gain	14 dBi
Polarization mismatch loss	0 dB
Miscellaneous jammer loss	2 dB
Jammer frequency coverage	200 MHz

B. SIMULATION RESULTS

Using the Razer Edge Pro tablet with the specifications outlined in Table 7, EAPPO produced the screenshots shown in Figures 30-34. Figure 30 and 31 screenshots demonstrate the mainlobe, sidelobes, and backlobe elevation and azimuth alignment calculations for the first point along the PE route. Any overlapping cell with the same color conveys elevation and azimuth alignment for the specific point and radar lobe. The screenshot shown in Figure 32 is an additional filter created to simulate the required distance separation between the PE and AEA platforms. The screenshot in Figure 33 is the jamming effectiveness data required output presented in Figure 2, with the darker green areas representing higher levels of jamming effectiveness giving AEA planners quantifiable jamming effectiveness to the mission strike leader. Finally, the screenshot in Figure 34 represents the EAPPO's final output to the AEA operator with the AEA optimized jamming route colored green. A complete video demonstration can be found at http://tgrteam.net/jammingvideo.html.

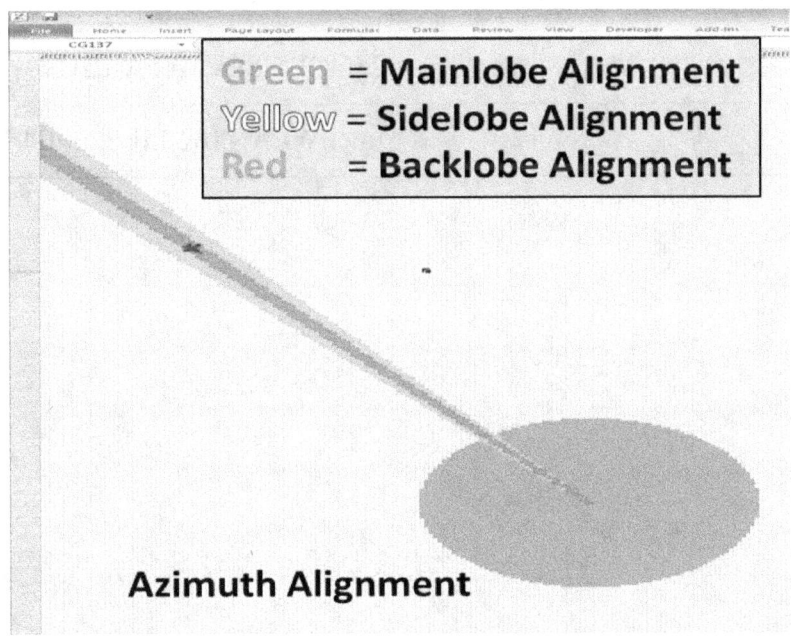

Figure 30. Screenshot depicting AEA location with azimuth alignment for the given PE location and a test emitter centered in the backlobe.

Table 7.   Razer Edge Pro Technical Specifications used to run the EAPPO software.

Computer Attribute	Manufacturer/Description
Maker	Razer
Model Name	Edge Pro
Processor	Intel Core i7 Dual core with Hyper Threading Base 1.9GHz /Turbo 3.0 GHz
Memory	8 GB DDR3 (1600MHz)
Video	Intel HD4000 (DX 11)
	NVIDIA GT 640M LE (2 GB DDR3)
Display	10.1" (IPS, 1366 X 768) Multi-touch HD display
Operating System	Windows 8
Storage	256 GB SSD (SATA-III)
Network	Intel WLAN (82.11b/g/n+BT4)

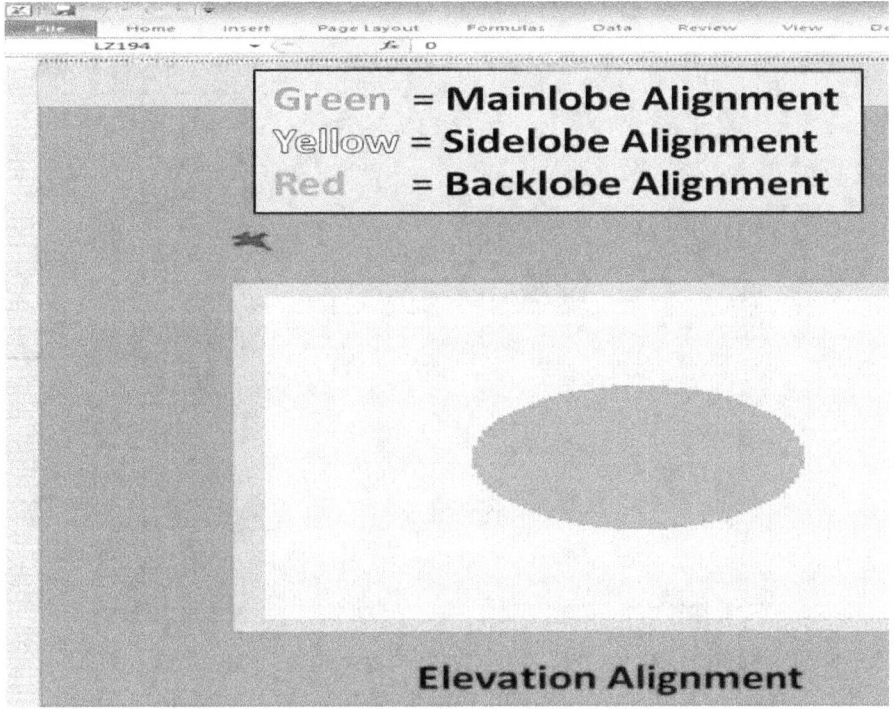

Figure 31.   Screenshot depicting AEA locations with elevation alignment for the given PE location and a test emitter centered in backlobe.

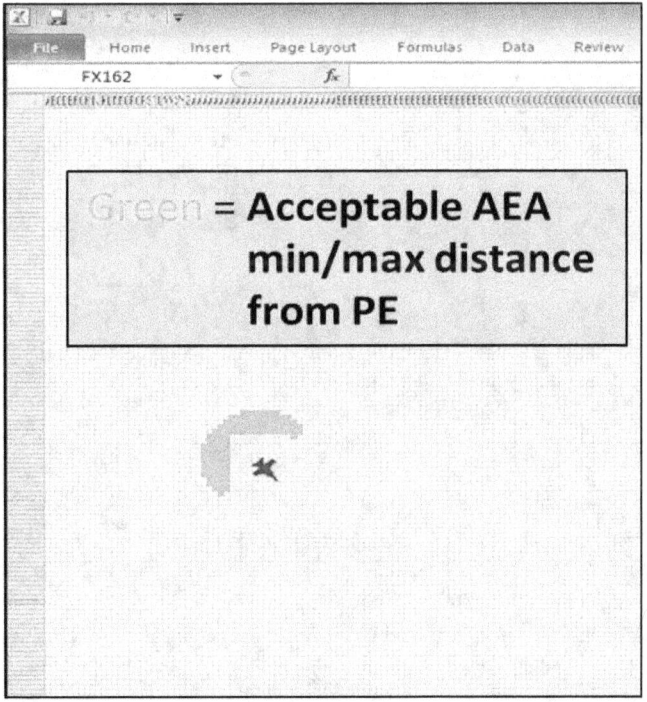

Figure 32.   Screenshot depicting AEA distance requirement (5-10 cells) from PE.

49

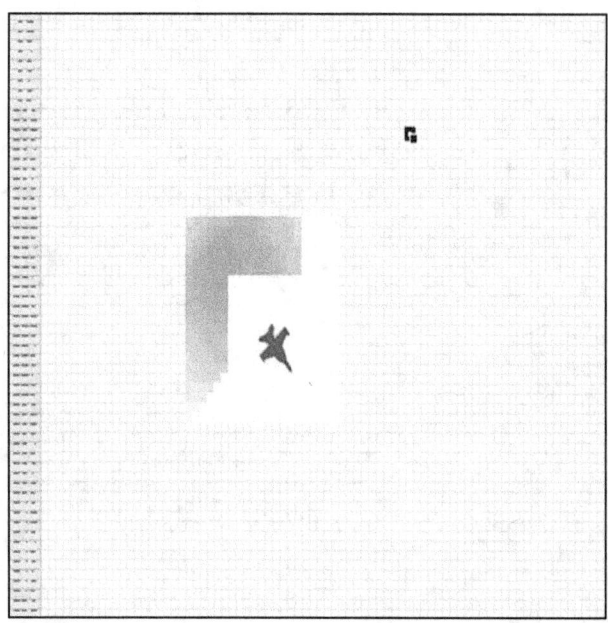

Figure 33. Screenshot depicting jamming effectiveness values at first PE point
in PE strike route.

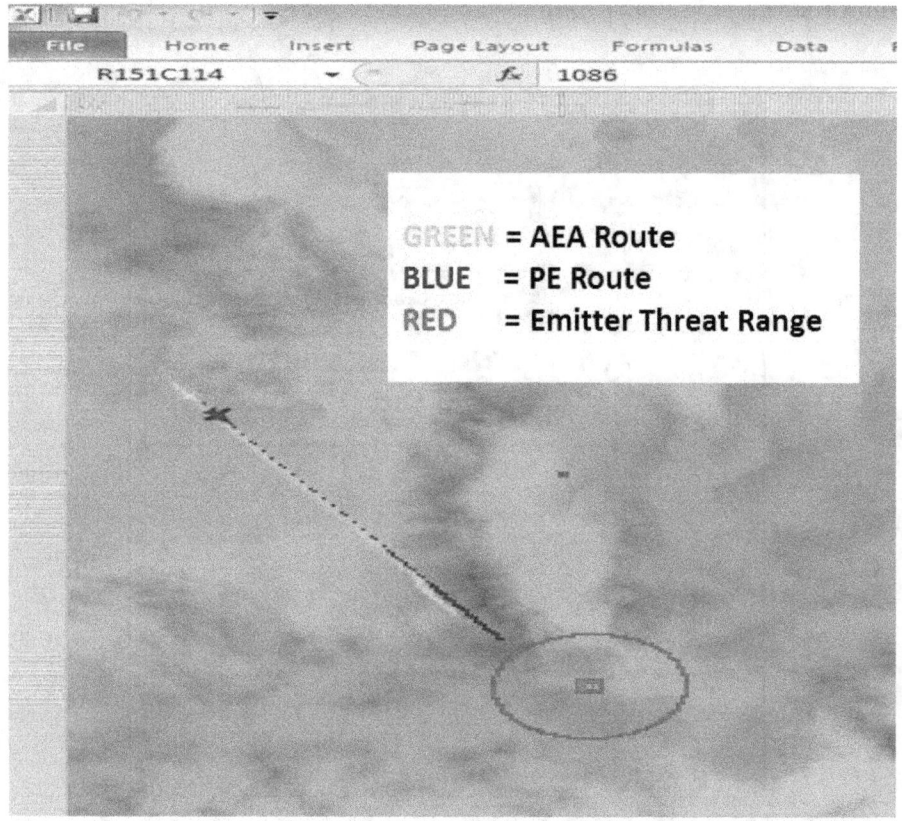

GREEN = AEA Route
BLUE = PE Route
RED = Emitter Threat Range

Figure 34. Final software results from software demonstrating automated
AEA route generation.

V. CONCLUSION AND RECOMMENDATIONS FOR FUTURE RESEARCH

A. CONCLUSION

Using only MS Office products, EAPPO proved the viability of creating complex military applications using only pre-approved software. The application developed is strictly for air platforms, but one can quickly see its applicability toward multiple other DOD requirements. Executed correctly, the proposed methodology should produce significant reductions in the time needed for software to meet the arduous DoD IA requirements.

Regardless of the reduced time to meet IA hurdles, applications such as the one developed in this thesis still needs to perform the complex testing and validation detailed in the DOD 5000. A more suitable requirement for use with the proposed methodology is to apply it toward non-mission critical applications such as presentations or laborious number crunching staff work, routinely conducted by headquarters staff and DOD employees. By the time automation software is introduced using traditional DOD software development techniques, the required reports may have changed or a new metric needed to be tracked, creating an infinite software development cycle where the changing requirements outpace the software deployment time, eventually requiring more resources to accomplish their intended tasks. Using preapproved software to automate tasks will help reverse this trend, potentially producing significant savings for the DOD. Ironically, using such an approach could also help the test and evaluation community itself, providing a method for development of low-cost, rapid prototyping of software designed to support specific testing evolutions/milestones/simulations.

B. RECOMMENDATIONS FOR FUTURE RESEARCH

1. Using the GPU from Excel

The methodology and algorithm applied in this thesis does not harness the tremendous capability of the GPU due to the constraints placed on the software development. Regardless, the parallel processing capability of the GPU can be used to

51

speed up computations. There are two foreseeable issues with programming the GPU: 1) security and 2) determining when the GPU is advantageous. Security is a problem applicable to all software development. With the GPU containing its own memory separate from the CPU, does it become less of a security liability? Also, the increased processing power of the GPU must offset the overhead of transferring data to and from the GPU. When are calculations performed on the GPU plus overhead faster than serial CPU calculations? More research is needed to properly answer these two questions.

2. Analysis of Using Web Browser versus Excel for Rendering Graphics

Although the methodology developed extensively uses MS Excel, other pre-approved software can potentially be used to develop EAPPO. For example, a web browser (Internet Explorer) is more suited for graphics compared to Microsoft Excel worksheet and is currently available on DOD networks. One could harness the web browser graphical libraries (WEBGL) from Microsoft VBA to produce commercial quality animation over Excel. Research is needed to provide a methodology for synchronizing the strengths of each individual application to completely harness the capabilities of using preapproved software.

3. Comparison of Linear versus Dynamic Programming for Optimization

Dynamic programming was chosen over linear programming when developing the EAPPO optimization algorithm. Research is needed to quantitatively determine the better method. Will increasing or decreasing the 2-D array size guide the optimization algorithm? Tests are needed to properly determine the selection of one method over the other.

4. Cyber Threat Analysis of Connecting Tablet to Aircraft

EAPPO assumes that the tablet can receive sensor data from the aircraft computer system. Can a computer be programmed to only allow for one-way communication to the tablet? Allowing two-way communication between the aircraft and tablet will introduce significant vulnerabilities and require extensive IA testing and validation. Providing that the communication port is strictly output only, the tablet could provide its own data filtering for real-time jamming and terrain impacted emitter range rings without the difficult and expensive tablet integration testing.

THIS PAGE INTENTIONALLY LEFT BLANK

APPENDIX

METHODOLOGY FOR USING GPU WITH EXCEL

Setting Up Excel:
1) Open Microsoft Excel 2010
2) Open VBA editor tool (Alt+F11)
3) Create a new module in workbook (Figure 1)
4) Declare dynamic memory in VBA (Figure1)
5) Declare external function on top of module with required input parameters
   a. Make sure the file path is correct. (Figure 1)
6) Call function using normal function call or sub routine procedures (Figure 2)

Create a CUDA compiled dynamically linked library (.dll) in Visual Studios
1) Create a new CUDA project (Figure 3)
2) Change configuration type of project to Dynamic Library.
3) Code Project
4) Create .def file (Can be skipped by using __declspec(dllexport) in function call) (Figure 4)
5) Build library (Figure 5)

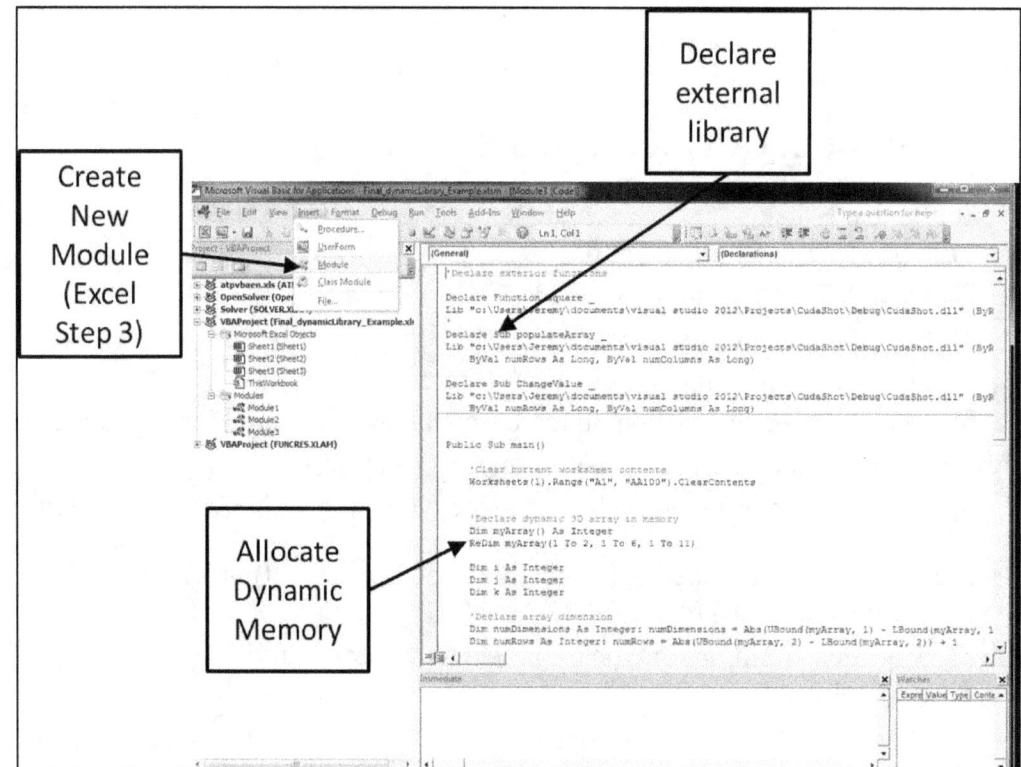

Figure 1.   Steps 3-5 of setting up EXCEL

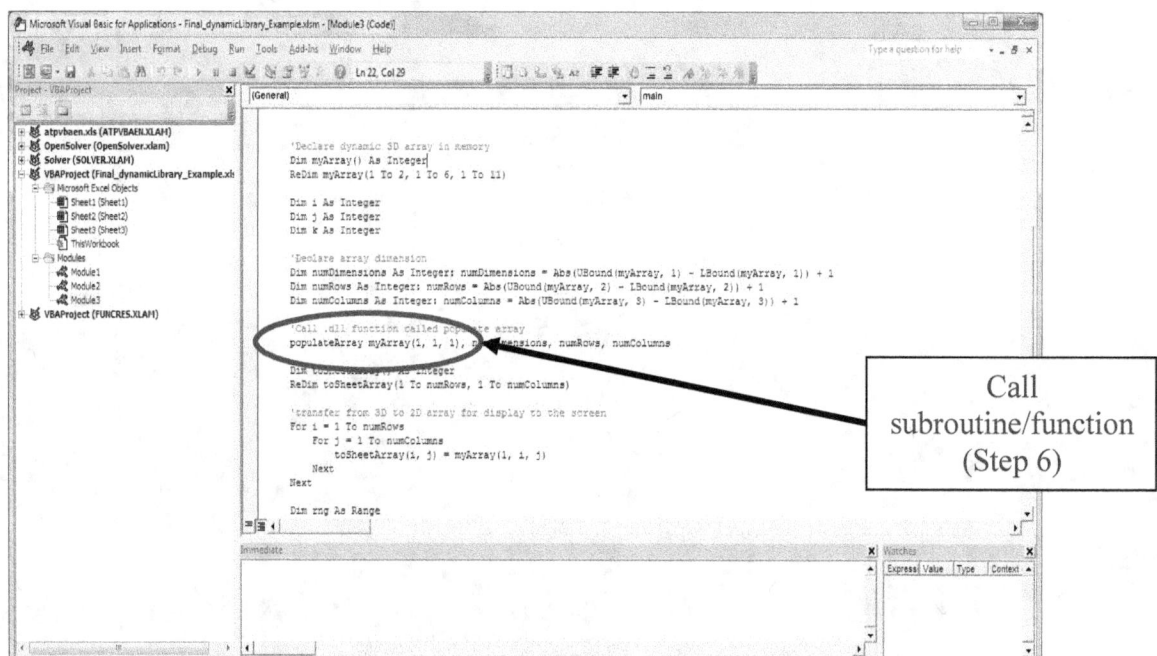

Figure 2.   STEP 6 of setting up EXCEL

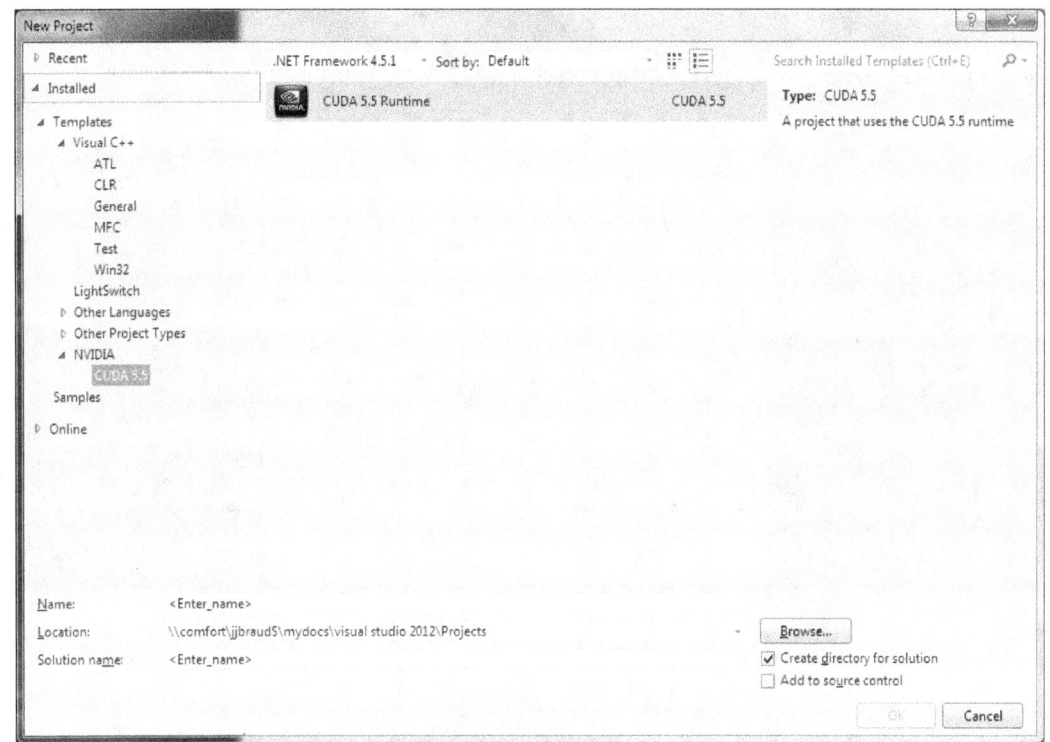

Figure 3.   Creating a new CUDA Project

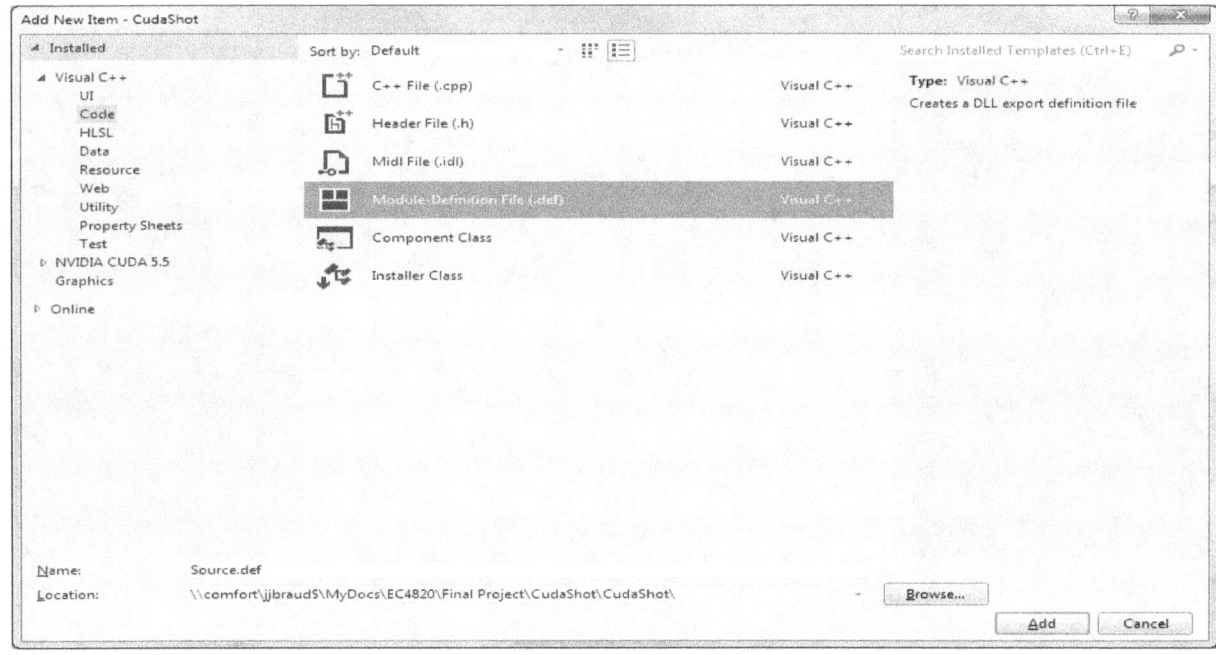

Figure 4.   Creating a .def file for use with .dll

57

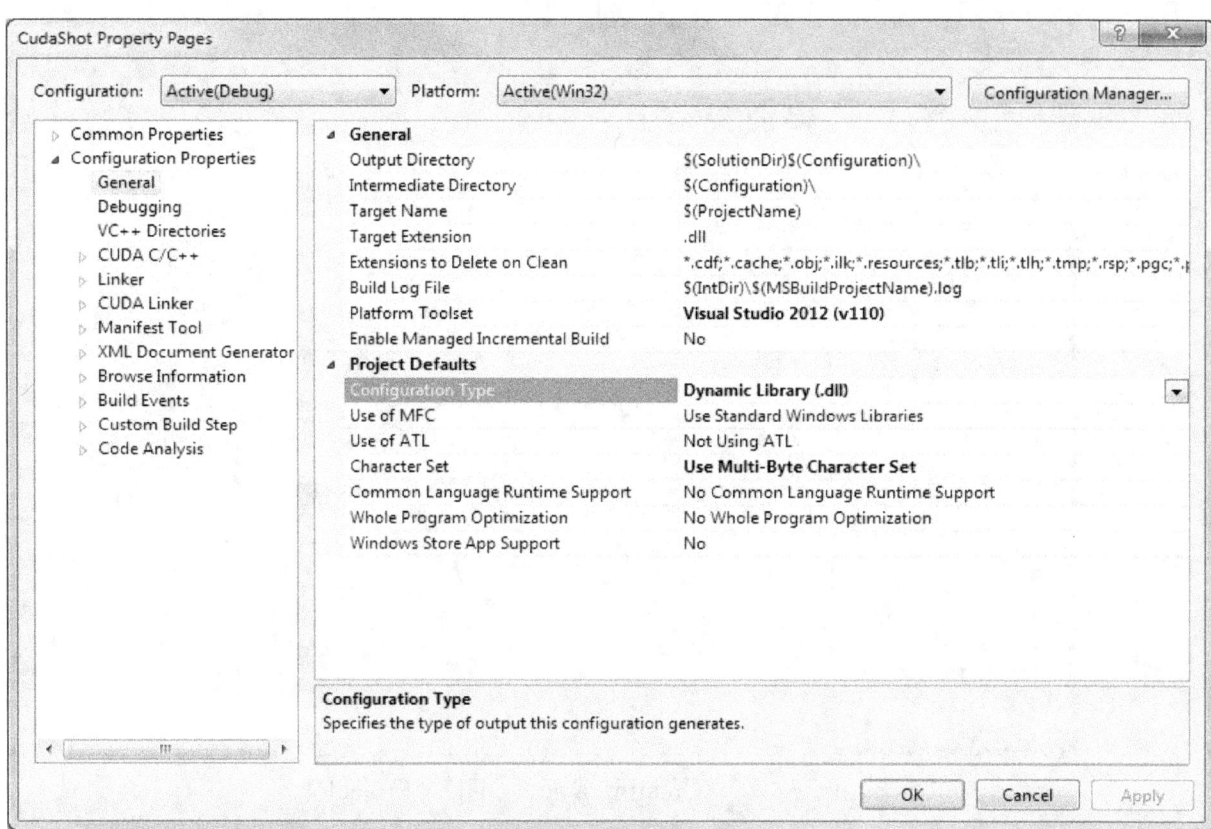

Figure 5.   Converting file from executable to library

LIST OF REFERENCES

[1]   *Performance Specification Digital Terrain Elevation Data (DTED)*, MIL-PRF-89020B, 2000.

[2]   K. Blattenberger. (n.d.). Electronic warfare and radar systems engineering handbook, Radar Horizon / Line of Sight - RF Café [Online]. Available: http://www.rfcafe.com/references/electrical/ew-radar-handbook/radar-horizon-line-of-sight.htm.

[3]   Bresenham line algorithm. (n.d.). *Wikipedia*. Available: http://en.wikipedia.org/wiki/Bresenham's_line_algorithm. Accessed Sep.14, 2014.

[4]   Dynamic replanning algorithm for aircrew display aid to assess jam effectiveness, by J. Dark et al., (2011, Feb. 22). *Patent Number 7893866* [Online]. Available: http://www.google.com/patents/US7893866.

[5]   J. E. Bresenham, "Algorithm for Computer Control of a Digital Plotter" *IBM Systems Journal,* vol. 4, no. 1, pp. 25–30, Jan. 1965.

[6]   E. Balas, "An Additive algorithm for solving linear programs with zero-one variables," *Operations Research,* vol. 13, no. 4, 517–546, July–Aug.1965.

[7]   J. Walkenback, *Microsoft Excel 2013 Power Programming with VBA*, Hoboken, NJ: John Wiley & Sons, 2013.

[8]   Application OnTime Method (Excel) [Online]. Available: http://msdn.microsoft.com/en-us/library/office/ff196165(v=office.15).aspx.

[9]   Berkeley sockets. (n.d.). *Wikipedia*. Available: http://en.wikipedia.org/wiki/Berkeley_sockets. Accessed Sept.14, 2014.